Evaluation research and social change

Evaluation research and social change

Alexander Weilenmann

unesco

Published in 1980 by the United Nations
Educational, Scientific and Cultural Organization
7 Place de Fontenoy, 75700 Paris
Printed by Snoeck-Ducaju & Son, Ghent (Belgium)

ISBN 92-3-101699-7

Preface

This publication is part of an ongoing activity of the Division for Socio-economic Analysis (Sector of Social Sciences and their Applications, Unesco) concerning the elaboration and promotion of the use of evaluation methods and techniques. Evaluation, in this context, is viewed as a social-science-based instrument of policy analysis, formulation and implementation.

Emphasis is primarily laid on strengthening capacity to carry out evaluation of social action projects in Member States of Unesco, the vast majority of which are in the developing world. The approach is multifaceted and includes, in addition to the conceptual work here presented, 'user' manuals, international symposia, regional seminars and national training workshops.

Evaluation Research has grown very rapidly in the last decade but within a rather restrictive and limited environment. Its potential, however, is intended to stimulate international dialogue in this growing but largely underdeveloped field of social science instrumentality.

Acknowledgements

Nguyen Van Hien, Zafar Iqbal Qureshi, Mohammed H. Sidky and Fred J. Sissine were active, stimulating, constructive collaborators in the preparation of this essay. The first three named made substantial contributions relating to aspects of development and development projects by reviewing and abstracting relevant literature and preparing cases. Their personal perspectives as members of the developing world, which they presented intelligently and critically, have been invaluable assets. Mr Sissine's primary contribution is reflected in the second chapter, the review of Evaluation Research literature. Moreover, the final version of this essay benefited from his critical analysis of preceding drafts.

Several of my colleagues read and commented on all or parts of an earlier draft, and I have benefited from discussions with them: Professors Ajay J. Creshkoff, Egbert deVries, William N Dunn, John Funari, Clifford C. Ham, Jr., and Thomas J. Pavlak. Mr Dunn gave of his knowledge and wisdom from the inception of this project; John Ratcliffe and Rabinder K. Sharma also helped in the initial formative stages.

While gratefully acknowledging the contributions of the collaborators and commentators mentioned above, I must also acknowledge my incapacity for doing full justice to their criticisms, suggestions and counsels. Without them, this essay would have been all the poorer; yet its deficiencies must be attributed to my own shortcomings.

A. W.

Contents

Introduction

In recent years, criticisms of, and expressions of dissatisfaction with, national and international socio-economic development efforts have increased in intensity and urgency and have penetrated major communication channels. What were but a few years ago the marginal voices of some Western critics and a few Third World intellectuals have become 'respectable' by and large and are being increasingly joined by the voices of mainstream institutions, scholars and practitioners. Development theory and the doctrines that guide development efforts have, since the days of the Marshall Plan for the reconstruction of Europe, exhibited shifts in emphasis. Basic assumptions and motivations of development policies are being increasingly questioned. The early understanding of development in terms of economic growth measured by the gross national product (or some similar standard) is shifting towards attention to the satisfying of basic human needs and the achieving of equity and opportunities for equality both within and between nations.

However, what has not emerged is a clearer understanding of what development entails. To the contrary, current discussion reflects uncertainty. Variety in the range of opinions, theories and doctrines concerning development and development policy has doubtless increased. But the search is unlikely to result in a new dominant model; rather, it seeks to replace the present one by alternative models that are expected to be rooted in the cultures to which they are to apply, instead of being imported from an alien culture.

At the same time, the urgency with which the need for social change and societal transformation is perceived in most of the developing world has not declined. The need for national societies to be able to cope with the conditions and circumstances of the time, to be capable of being themselves and of enjoying dignity and integrity, is growing more acute as time passes. The vehicle for effecting social change and societal transformation[1] is the project or projects. In other words, things do not happen by themselves;

for change and transformation to take place, organized activity is essential.[2] Indeed, national governments and international agencies invest considerable funds in development projects in the expectation that the project activities will make a difference with respect to 'development' and to the nature and well-being of the society and its people. The present essay is concerned with this kind of project, i.e. projects that are intended to effect social change and societal transformation; projects that are designed for immediate, narrow purposes—such as emergency relief projects or experimental pilot projects—are not specifically considered. Moreover, in a very general sense, the focus of attention is on rural development projects, rather than those in an urban or industrial context. This distinction, however, is informal and as such not very important, given the level of abstraction of this essay.

If projects are to effect social change and societal transformation, the question will arise: What change and what kind of societal transformation?[3] Any intervention is likely to bring about social change and may contribute to some societal transformation. Indeed, the literature is replete with accounts of undesirable change as a consequence of a project. Theory and doctrine, with their assumptions and values, speak of the kind of social change that is desired, and establish the linkage between project activity and societal change and transformation. But when there are several theories and many doctrines, when underlying assumptions and values are modified, it is not at all clear what sort of social change should be brought about and in what the societal transformation should consist. This is the problem of development policy and project planning; it is also the problem of the evaluation of the project and its impacts.

The purpose of this essay is to develop and suggest a methodology of evaluating development projects and their impacts on, and contributions to, social change and societal transformation. The concept of evaluation implies the matching of, or comparison between, values and goal images on the one hand and actual or anticipated outcomes on the other.

Thus, in addition to being able to describe, monitor, and anticipate the course of events initiated by a project activity, which is the general task of the social sciences and of historiography, evaluation involves also the identification and specification of criteria with which effects can be matched and compared. The thrust of the preceding paragraphs, which will be elaborated upon in Chapter 1, is that the nature and properties of such criteria are not necessarily given and may never be completely and definitely specified. Rather, they are subject to continuous change, such that the image of a dialectical process becomes relevant; stress and strain, conflict and tension permeate the situation.

Traditional social science, including evaluation research derived from it, tends to assume that problem situations are well structured and that there is a 'truth' which can in principle be discovered. In contrast, more recent views hold that most non-trivial social situations are ill-structured (Churchman,

1968, 1971; Mitroff, 1974), and that most social problems are 'messes' (Ackoff, 1974*a,b*) inasmuch as problems are interrelated and no one can be solved by itself in isolation from others. Modern science has also become more careful about assuming that there is a 'truth', a 'law' that can in principle be discovered; rather, any manifestation or phenomenon is seen as one possibility in a range of possible manifestations or phenomena. The simple cause-and-effect relationship, which traditional social science tends doggedly to pursue, is then virtually impossible and nonsensical. Nevertheless, in the real world of policy, planning and administration, decisions must be made and impacts must be evaluated. The present essay attempts to make a contribution to the resolution of this dilemma.

The comparison of goal values with effects is a prominent theme of cybernetics. A system would be 'blind' if it were not able to evaluate information about the effects of its previous action. Evaluation research and analysis is an intellectual task necessary for viable decision-making on a continuous basis, rather than a discrete activity that has a definite beginning and a definite end. If the distinction between 'formative' and 'summative' evaluation, which is often drawn in current literature, makes sense in the present context, this essay will have to settle on formative evaluation—but not so much with respect to the project as with respect to the societal system.[4] Project impacts may continue even when the project as such has long since been discontinued.

The concept of system and the cybernetic perspective call attention to the condition of circularity and the network characteristic of social phenomena. Social situations are full of mutual causal relationships, where A affects B and B affects A. Again, the simple, undirectional cause-and-effect assumption is largely inappropriate. Given a relatively complex situation, the 'causes' cannot be completely enumerated and specified. Traditional social science offers few methods and techniques to get at such situations and tends to ignore them.

In brief, this essay and its methodology seek to cope with, rather than shirk, such conditions as complexity, ill-structuredness, circularity, and network effect. The methodology to be developed may be somewhat unconventional. Compared with traditional approaches, it requires a new mode of thinking and of posing questions. Some issues that have become important in traditional social science and Evaluation Research[5] recede into the background and others are being emphasized. It should be stressed that this essay does not engage in evaluation. Rather, it seeks to suggest how one might engage in evaluating development-project impacts. It develops a methodology; i.e. its subject-matter is concerned with a logic of inquiry and focuses on structuring the problem of how one might go about evaluating the impact of development projects on social change and societal transformation.

This essay does not offer a 'manual' of project evaluation. It is not intended for the practising evaluator whose task is largely circumscribed by the institutional context in which he finds himself. It does not address itself directly to the level of operating concerns. Rather, it is intended for those persons in national and international agencies who are in a position to affect, guide and facilitate such policies and strategies. Its intended readership includes those who seek to mediate between theory and practice, between conceptualization and operation, and who are to be found in national and international development agencies, as well as in academe and other organizations.

One of the specific tasks to be dealt with in this essay relates to the question of linking project activities with the much broader context of social change and societal transformation. Chapter 1 begins with this broader context. If projects are to be evaluated from the point of view of their impacts on social change and societal transformation, it will be necessary to establish evaluation criteria in terms of questions about social change and societal transformation. In other words, change manifestations need to be assessed as to the values they satisfy or do not satisfy. Chapter 1 demonstrates the ill-structuredness, the fuzziness of the development situation by sketching the changes which theories and doctrines that seem fundamental to development policy have undergone over time. The reader will also be exposed to some critical concepts that are used in the essay.

Chapter 2 reviews critically the prevailing Evaluation Research literature and, in a sense, tells why this essay needed to be written.

The third chapter seeks to fulfil two purposes. On the one hand, it offers a conceptualization of society and its processes that lead to decisions concerning social change and societal transformation. On the other hand, the reader is expected to become somewhat familiar with an approach to conceptually organized social systems. The same approach will then be used again and applied to the project as a social system. Chapter 4 focuses on the project and its relations with environmental parts. The two chapters together constitute the conceptual-methodological foundation for an evaluation methodology in the present context. Each from a different direction—top down, and bottom up—and both derived from social systems' cybernetics, the two chapters furnish the intellectual tools with which a methodology is fashioned for the purpose at hand.

The fifth chapter then guides the reader through the evaluation methodology towards which the previous chapters have been building.

Notes

1. Throughout this essay, a distinction is made between 'social' and 'societal'. The former term, 'social', is a short form of 'socio-cultural' (Buckley, 1967), i.e. those processes and events that characterize and are characterized by human activities

resulting from interaction of man with man and his non-human resources, including political, economic, etc., as well as cultural concerns and manifestations. It does not imply any particular level of analysis or aggregation and can refer to a small group as much as to a nation and supranational society. The term 'societal' refers to a relatively totipotential (Miller, 1978) socio-cultural system, i.e. a socio-cultural system that has some degree of autonomy and decision-making capability; it is usually bound spatially and characterized by politico-administrative organization. The term tends to refer to national society within national State borders. Yet, it may also refer to subnational regions as socio-cultural systems, in those cases where national society can be 'naturally' decomposed into socio-cultural regional systems of reasonable autonomy. Other possible referents for 'societal', such as multinational or transnational society, or the society of a city, are less relevant in the context of this essay.

2. Things do, or may, happen 'by themselves' i.e. without organized, planned activity. But then they happen haphazardly, and it is much more difficult to steer the course of events. History may have been a process exhibiting a relatively high degree of randomness; but the future seems considerably too risky compared with the entire past of mankind. The human being might as well use his or her intelligence for self-control.
3. The term 'societal transformation' is preferred in this context to 'development'. The former carries with it fewer connotations and denotations than the latter.
4. Like much of prevailing evaluation research methodology, the two concepts were introduced in the context of educational curriculum evaluation. 'Formative' evaluation occurs while the activity to be evaluated is going on and helps to improve or direct it. In contrast, 'summative' evaluation assesses a finished product, such as a curriculum, with respect to its effectiveness and potential for further adoptions (cf. Weiss, 1972).
5. The capital initials, E and R, indicate that reference is made to the somewhat formalized, institutionalized methodology that goes under this label—in contrast to a generically conceived intellectual task. The distinction is not hard and fast; the Evaluation Research is also evolving. See Chapter 2.

1 On social change and societal transformation

In considering the two concepts of social change and societal transformation, there is no intention here to develop a full-fledged 'theory' of social change and transformation. The treatment is eclectic, presumably appropriate for the topic at hand.

One way of thinking about reasons for social change and societal transformation is to say that a society and any of its parts have a need to cope[1] with their social and physical environments or, more precisely, with relevant changes in their environments. Thus, in this view, society undergoes socio-cultural changes and transforms itself in order to increase the probability of its playing out its character (Deutsch, 1966*a*), of remaining itself, and of fulfilling its fundamental purpose. The difficulty is that it is not at all clear in what this coping consists, what constitutes the society's character and fundamental purpose, and what sorts of social change are desirable and necessary for coping. This difficulty arises in the case of any one specific society, as well as when more generic theory-building is attempted across societies. Different people in any one society are likely to perceive their society's environment differently and to advocate and support different strategies for coping. Similarly, different societies are apt to place different emphases on environmental events and their internal structures. The framework will have to take this situation into account and avoid speculating and stipulating a priori what is 'good' for a society.

What has been sketched above is characteristic of 'ill-structured' problem situations.[2] The term suggests that a problem does not have one, definite, straightforward solution. Rather, any solution depends on how the problem is structured, that is, on the assumptions—which in turn reflect values and goal images and affect other values and goal images—that are brought to bear on the problem situation. Specifically, an ill-structured problem obtains when two (or more) conflicting value structures and goal images characterize the situation. It can safely be said that most social-problem situations can be approached with different sets of values and goal images, although one of them may in fact dominate the others and prevail. Indeed, power-holders tend to view problem situations as well-structured and are satisfied that their own values and goal images are the pertinent ones. All too often, ill-structured problems are treated as if they were well-structured. People in charge, decision-makers, theorists and practitioners may not realize that the assumptions they bring to the problem are not the only ones possible, and they fail to recognize that the assumptions are not shared by others who also have a stake in the decision outcomes, that is, in the problem resolution. In order to optimize problem solutions, different and conflicting sets of assumptions should be identified and confronted with each other (cf. Mitroff and Featheringham, 1974; Mitroff and Sagasti, 1973).

Prevailing theories of social change and development have tended to treat their phenomena as 'well-structured' problem situations, each attempting to establish, if not claiming to have established, the conditions for and the essence of social change and development. A review of the literature reveals that the assumptions, values and goal images pertaining to social change and development have evolved with time, and so have the theories, doctrines and strategies.

Although one of the principal organs of the United Nations, the Economic and Social Council, has included a reference to 'social' in its name since the inception of the organization, and although non-economic Specialized Agencies, such as Unesco, are of long standing, it has been difficult for theorists, experts and governmental practitioners to deal with development outside an economic perspective that emphasizes economic growth. Economic growth—as manifested, for example, in increased gross national product—was the dominant criterion and policy thrust, and development projects of any kind were expected to contribute to the country's economic growth. Cost-benefit analysis in monetary terms was the corollary. Subsequently, theorizing shifted to the recognition of other categories, general social, political and psychological variables, which were thought to enhance economic growth. Social indicators increasingly supplemented economic indicators, and the two categories were correlated with each other and factor-analysed (e.g. Adelman and Morris, 1967). From lists of such indicators, it can be inferred which factors, categories and events seem to be considered important in the social-change and development processes. Causality in the relationships of variables is claimed to be established by correlational, regression and similar modes of analysis.

More recently, perspectives seem to have been shifting, and new value assumptions are becoming more prevalent. Not only are old criteria replaced by new ones, but the ill-structuredness of the problem situation is becoming more apparent. While a concept such as economic growth applies to an aggregate, 'quality of life' pertains to individuals, and the questions arise: Whose life? What quality? Disappointment with past strategies based on economic growth have become prevalent, and the notion of development is increasingly associated with concerns such as equity, basic needs and quality of life. While there has been the more or less explicit hope that an increase in gross national product will eventually produce a more equitable distribution of income and wealth, it is now suggested that the causality may be reversed: increased GNP may possibly result from greater equity. Such a reversal of priorities affects any assessment of the significance of manifestations of social change and societal transformation.

One of the most recent attempts at determining the state of national development is the Physical Quality of Life Index, which combines measures of life expectancy at birth, infant mortality, and literacy rates (Morris and Liser, 1977). Designed to replace such indicators as GNP and GNP per capita, the new index reflects the desire to get at manifestations of socio-economic (and perhaps socio-cultural) well-being that matter in a wider context of social morality and are correlated with other indicators that are thought to be significant.

It is clear, however, that all of these efforts assume or imply a well-structured problem situation, however complex it may be and however much uncertainty may be associated with it. In this respect, these modern attempts are not so different from the alchemists' belief in being able to find the precise concoction that would transform base metal into gold and lead to everlasting happiness.

Before presenting a framework that accounts for ill-structuredness, another aspect of the concept of change and transformation needs to be touched upon. Change may be continuous over a considerable period of time. However, it may also be discontinuous. Prevailing theories of social change tend to assume or imply continuity of change, which is reflected in the preferred notion of growth. A graph that does not show a monotonic increase, preferably at an exponential rate, is suspect or, rather, the activities represented by the graph are suspect. Sigmoid or S-shaped curves, often called growth curves, are, of course well known and have been associated with various manifestations of growth and change. Yet, discontinuities in change processes have found virtually no reflection in the general literature. Some mathematical treatments allow for step functions; but in general theory and method have largely been helpless in the face of manifest discontinuities.[3] Recent developments in 'catastrophe theory' (Holt *et al,* 1978; Thom, 1975; Zahler and Sussman, 1977; Zeeman, 1976) promise to provide practical tools to explain the model discontinuities, and they have provided a deepening of insights into 'sudden' change. Such developments reinforce the view that theories of equilibrium and disequilibrium are not suited to dealing effectively with the dynamics of social change (cf. Gross, 1966; Deutsch, 1966*a*), except to describe temporary states of components of the system, in contrast with the system as a whole. Similarly, it has often been perceived and expressed—though not systematically studied—that the accumulation of small, barely perceptible changes over time may result in a major change involving fundamental structural change (Deutsch and Merritt, 1965; Gross, 1966). The assumption that a project should result in continuous growth leads to one of two reactions when the expected growth slackens or stops, each of which may be inappropriate (Moore, 1977). The decision may be to abandon the project as an activity that is not worthwhile, or it may be decided to 'save' the project by increasing the effort and resource inputs. Moreover, the assumption of continuity favours short-term planning.

The preceding discussion of discontinuities in change processes is particularly pertinent in the context of this book, which is concerned with societal transformation. The word transformation refers to 'big' change, to change that manifestedly makes a difference. Historians have been able to identify transformations in the grand scheme of history. They have reason, at least in the context of European history, to consider societies after the year 1500 to be significantly different from the same societies before that threshold. Over a period of about two hundred years the Industrial Revolution has transformed the world and made it what it is today; in spite of the prominence of the word 'industrial' the changes that characterize this transformation have been manifold. Today industrialized societies are being transformed into post-industrial societies; we, contemporaries, are not quite certain what this entails, but can sense, and have itemized indications, that major fundamental changes are taking place and that some tomorrow will be quite distinct from today. Yes, and we learn, theorize and plan about 'development', a transformation that the non-industrialized societies are undergoing, or are expected to undergo, or want to undergo. However, collectively, we are not certain what this transformation may look like, what the transformed processes and structures may be. We are about as uncertain about the transformation of development as we are about the transformation from industrialized to post-industrial society. There is a difference between the two transformations: the latter one is essentially casual; it is, at best, steered so as to avoid undesirable consequences on a case-to-case basis, so to speak. The development transformation, in contrast, is perceived to be urgent; it is planned, almost forced; it threatens to be entirely 'artificial'. Except to satisfy our curiosity, we do not need a clear image of post-industrial society, although society could do a better job of improving itself if it knew where it was going. The planned, purposive transformation of development should have an image of the post-developing state of affairs. But, as was pointed out earlier in this chapter, while there are images, there is no image; there are value structures, but no value structure; there are goal sets, but no goal set.

Again, we may look at development theories and their underlying assumptions (cf. Chodak, 1973). A long tradition of development theory is based on assumptions about the evolution of human society that are supposed to be universally applicable. Representatives of this kind of theorizing include Comte, Spencer, Marx and most of his followers, Tönnies, Max

Weber, Alfred Weber, and contemporaries such as Parsons and Smelser. Although differentially recognizing variations, they all look upon development as going through stages, each of which has specific characteristics that are schematically formulated and furnish the rationale for classificatory, explanatory and predictive measurement. While they may claim universality, these theories cannot deny their European background. A critical consequence of this perspective is the assumption that developing societies must go through the stages that industrialized, i.e. European, society has already experienced.

In its consequences closely related to the evolutionary assumption, another theoretical stream regards development as a transformation into 'modernization'. In this perspective, the most 'advanced' societies, the most industrialized and modern ones, constitute the model for development and provide an image of where the transformation is headed, at least to the extent that industrialized society is understood in its varied manifestations. And to the extent that it is understood what has made industrialized society industrial, the causal factors and conditions for development toward modernization can be inferred. Levy, Bendix, Eisenstadt, Apter are primary examples of theorists of modernization. Max Weber discovered the conditions for modern life and resorted to psychological, attitudinal variables. McClelland's need-achievement motivation stems from similar roots, as does Hagan's 'status withdrawal'.

One implication of such approaches is that there are people who know, or believe they know, and determine what modernization consists of and who set the objectives and strategies of development. Planning is centralized, and the centres of decision require obedience and conformity on the part of the society at large. This is doubtless a mode of operation that is ill suited in ill-structured problem situations.

A third category of approaches is characterized by reliance on theory about basic human and social processes. This kind of theorizing seeks to identify and specify requirements for fundamental social change derived from insights about the nature of man and of human behaviour. The discourse tends to be more concrete, but also more fragmented, than the discourse of the theorists of evolution and modernization. For instance, Deutsch's (1961, 1966*b*) concept of social mobilization asks what happens when new population clusters are exposed to streams of information and are thus mobilized into the societal network. The underlying assumptions are those of theories of social communication and of an essentially cybernetic perspective of society. With due care about avoiding various fallacies and logical traps, it may be concluded that conditions of social mobilization are prerequisites for including the whole population of the societal (national) space into the active society. Theory may (and does) suggest that a society that has mobilized its entire population and is continuing the mobilization process is probably more viable in the contemporary era than a society that includes large clusters of non-mobilized populations. The next step would then be to devise development policies that ensure social mobilization. The manifestations of and the conditions for social mobilization may differ from society to society. Most empirically oriented social scientists, including names mentioned previously, belong to this category at one time or another. The assumptions underlying such approaches pertain to a lower level of abstraction than is the case in the first two categories. In principle, they offer opportunities for accumulating insights concerning social change and societal transformation that are relevant for specific policy situations and configurations.

The purpose of the preceding paragraphs has not been a presentation of a history of development theory and doctrine or a review of such theories and doctrines. Rather, their purpose has been to demonstrate in principle the presence of a large variety of assumptions that tend to go into development theory and associated policy-formation. Any decision affecting social change and societal transformation has a wide choice among different and often conflicting value and goal assumptions. However, all too often, the assumptions are not recognized as such. Instead, planning and policy-making derive from what particular decision-makers consider to be the appropriate values and assumptions in accordance with their current world views, to the extent that they are aware of them at all. They are missing the opportunity for widening the range and variety of assumptions, values and goal images that might enter decision-making, and are thus limiting the variety of possible outcomes.

Notes

1. In the present context, the term 'coping' is preferred to 'adapting' for semantic reasons. The latter term is often misunderstood as implying passivity, subordination, dependence on the part of a system *vis-à-vis* its environment. But an offensive attack on the enemy is one way of adapting to (or coping with) the environment.
2. In addition to Churchman (1968, 1971), Mitroff (1974), and Ackoff (1974*a,b*), cited in the introduction, Maruyama's (1977) 'heterogenistic' epistemology conveys a similar idea.
3. For instance, a well-known and prominent mathematical text on social change (Hamblin *et al,* 1973) refers to Robert Nisbet's criticism of earlier work which assumed that all social change occurred gradually and continuously from uniform causes endogenous to the society or culture in question. While the authors of the mathematical text promise to be able to take into account both endogenous and exogenous variables, they ignore Nisbet's reference to the continuity assumption.

2 A critical review of Evaluation Research literature

As Chapter 1 has demonstrated, development-problem situations tend to be ill-structured and can be characterized as messes. The present chapter seeks to inquire how the prevailing Evaluation Research methodology might cope with such problem situations. Moreover, possibilities of linking specific project activities and impacts with the broader context of social change and societal transformation need to be investigated. The purpose of this chapter is thus to review the body of literature that can be, and has been, identified as Evaluation Research and reflects a profession with somewhat institutionalized practices and a definite, although continuously evolving, methodology. The intellectual activity of evaluating policies, programmes and projects, as well as socio-cultural institutions, has presumably been going on ever since man began to make conscious decisions and wondered whether one course of action was 'better' than another one. But it required a configuration of circumstances for this activity to become systematized and institutionalized as a distinct scholarly and professional concern.[1] The basic question to be asked in this chapter is whether and to what extent the concerns of Evaluation Research match the concerns of this essay. In other words, this chapter should not be read as a general critique of Evaluation Research. The purpose of the review is limited specifically to its possible use in meeting the requirements of the task dealt with in this essay.

The present review is organized into a section dealing with 'classical' Evaluation Research, and a section treating contemporary efforts. A third section considers 'social-impact assessment', a relatively recent development independent of the mainstream of Evaluation Research. As in the case of social change and development theory, it must be pointed out that a chronological classification contains its own seeds of falsification. Earlier contributions are not necessarily replaced by later efforts. Rather, different trends often occur simultaneously in parallel with slight shifts in current emphasis. Newer methodological problems, methods and techniques tend to be discussed in the literature more frequently than older ones, although the latter may continue to prevail in practice. For reasons of practicality, it has been necessary to review the literature, rather than the practice, of Evaluation Research. A recent review of evaluative reports concerning development projects (Bachrach, 1977) will be referenced at the end of the second section.

'Classical' Evaluation Research

As a somewhat formal field of inquiry, Evaluation Research is the child of social-science research as it developed in the 1950s and early 1960s in the United States. To be slightly blunt, social science had discovered 'science'; i.e. it had adopted a positivist, empiricist stance and had acquired rigorous methods and techniques that were thought to ensure validity and reliability of research findings. This 'scientific' social-science research forswore any consideration of values and sought to conduct 'science' as a value-free enterprise. There was no place for evaluation, which required a normative attitude; at best, it could characterize and monitor social processes and structural change.

But at about the time when social scientists had mastered scientific tools, the United States Government engaged heavily in social-welfare programmes, many of which were of an experimental nature and needed evaluation. The expenditure of large sums had to be justified, and people—from taxpayers to local and state officials to legislators—had to be persuaded that these programmes did what they promised to do. Scholars and practitioners associated with the professions of education and social work began to devote themselves to the task of demonstrating the success of public-service programmes. Early attempts consisted in administering self-rating appraisal forms and promulgating 'evaluation guides'. The devising of questionnaires and their administration to programme participants continues to be a favoured tool for evaluating participants' satisfaction with the programme; unfortunately, all too often, much too much is read into this primitive tool by programme managers. Evaluation came to be considered to be a function in and by itself, separate from the functions of programme planning and programme implementation. It was done—and much of it is still being done today—upon the termination of a programme or when requests for programme renewal had to be justified. Functional separability and *ex post facto* designs tend to go hand in hand. The former is reflected in the professionalization of Evaluation Research, which seeks an entry into planning and implementation, as will be discussed below, the latter is the subject of much methodological dissatisfaction and has given rise to the search for greater methodological sophistication on the part of the Evaluation Research community.[2]

Given the state of 'scientific' social science in the 1960s, issues concerning the quality of Evaluation Research with respect to reliability and validity became acute. The solution was found in the theory of experimental design. The response to the demand for a methodologically sound approach was to emphasize the use of reliable and valid methods and techniques for measuring goal-directed effects. Much of this movement was an attempt at standardizing measures of programme effectiveness. Thus, 'classical' Evaluation Research basically assumed (a) that programme goals could be identified and specified in unambiguous terms, (b) that they could be translated into measurable indicators of goal achievement, (c) that experimental design principles (particularly relating to control groups that did not receive the 'treatment') could be applied, (d) that data on the indicators for both the experimental and control groups were in fact available, or could be generated, and (e) that the data on programme participants and control groups could be compared in terms of goal criteria (cf. Weiss, 1972*b*). This approach makes the overall assumption that the problem situation is characterized by clear measurement criteria and unambiguous data sources. It is the contention of the preceding chapters of this essay that these conditions are not fulfilled in the context in question. They are rarely fulfilled, indeed, in the situations which Evaluation Research tends to be concerned with, i.e. specific social-welfare, including educational, programmes.

Indeed, a number of problems became apparent and have occupied the Evaluation Research literature ever since. One such problem was the tension between evaluator and administrator, the problem of the balance between the administrator's needs and those of the evaluator. The conflict was over the criteria for programme success. The evaluator emphasized improvement of the status of programme service recipients, and the administrator tended to emphasize smoothness and efficiency of the services. In the language of this essay, multiple perspectives entered relevant goal images and, thus, goal criteria. While the evaluator's degree of confidence in his findings increased because of the infusion of scientific criteria for evaluation, the administrative criteria largely determined the utilization of the research findings, and under-utilization of findings became a serious problem for Evaluation Research. At this stage, at least, the need for scientific rigour and for applying scientifically proper methods and techniques dominated Evaluation Research that was not prepared to abandon the assumption of the well-structured problem situation (cf. Suchman, 1967; Weiss, 1972*a*, Chapter 6).

Another problem that arose involved the interpretation of small or negative programme effects. They could be explained in two different ways, which created ambiguity and affected research utilization. One side argued that experimental design principles were not fully adhered to in the research; the explanation was thus sought in the conduct of evaluative inquiry. Indeed, it was often difficult to make random assignments in the populations and/or to apply other statistical control procedures to protect the design from validity threats. The temptation was great to select those outcome indicators for investigation that could be measured the most accurately and manipulated the most conveniently for statistical analysis—to the detriment of other factors that might have been more meaningful in the problem situation.

The second explanation of small or negative programme effects did not question the inquiry, but suggested that programmes were not adequately implemented; the criticism was thus levelled at the conduct of the programme goal-directed activities. This second concern gave rise to a branch of Evaluation Research that focused on studying the programme's processes, rather than its goal achievement (cf. Rossi, 1972). This development constituted a shift away from the classical model—but by no means its substitution—and may be considered as a broadening of the philosophical basis of Evaluation Research. The purpose of process evaluation is to guide the ongoing programme activities and to provide information needed to refocus and redirect programme goals in response to and in anticipation of changes in the programme's target environment. The activities of process evaluation as 'formative' evaluation could be intimately intertwined with programme activities and become an additional source and catalyst of programme impacts. In the last analysis, the final programme outcomes are inseparable from the effects of evaluative inputs made during the course of programme implementation.

In the case of formative evaluation, scientific rigour and strict adherence to the principles of experimental design are considered to be of little importance (Weiss, 1972*a*), if only because of political and practical obstacles. For the same reason, formative evaluation is looked down upon by the classical purists, who concentrate on the evaluation of a programme's goal-attainment. A methodology asking only questions of goal-attainment becomes concerned solely with problems of data reliability and the validity of inferences, neglecting problems of data interpretation that emerge from a methodology asking also about implementation and goal changing. The former tends to lack the capacity of combining concerns for research quality with administrative concerns. This, in turn raises the problem of research utilization that is determined by administrative concerns (cf. Gilbert *et al.*, 1975; Bennet and Lumsdaine, 1975).

The ideal of process evaluation is to make repeated evaluations and measurements during a programme's operating life. On the other hand, the ideal of the classical impact model is to assess conditions before and after the programme's life span. But there is no a priori reason to believe that programme impacts cease with the termination of a programme. Generally speaking, the effects of social and technological innovations diffuse slowly throughout society, sometimes lasting for years and even decades. Thus, an argument can be made for repeated measurements of programme impact after the completion of the programme. Both practical and methodological problems—virtually insurmountable ones from the point of view of the methodological assumptions and aspirations of classical Evaluation Research—cause serious obstacles to follow-up research for periods of time after the completion of a programme. An early appeal for repeated measurements over time after the completion of a programme was made by Hayes (1959) in the context of evaluating development projects. It does not seem that his appeal has met with a strong response.

The difficulties that classical Evaluation Research encountered, particularly in the area of research utilization, and the continued search for precision and validity, created sufficient tension for the Evaluation Research community to adopt new perspectives. These will be discussed in the next section.

Contemporary Evaluation Research

Contemporary Evaluation Research methodology admits the classical assumptions, yet refines them and adapts them to the growing perception of the social world's complexity. Perhaps more consciously than, say, ten years ago, Evaluation Research today is seen as applied social science. Or, to put it the other way round, applied social science has again become more generally accepted as a legitimate expression of social-science endeavour, and theorists and practitioners of Evaluation Research feel freer to identify themselves as applied social scientists. At the same time, the professionalization and institutionalization of the activity have advanced, with organizations, conferences and periodicals, as well as textbooks, anthologies, handbooks and annuals. Moreover, Evaluation Research is done through a variety of organizational arrangements, including—in the United States—profit-making and non-profit organizations, governmental and semi-governmental agencies, university institutes and centres, all the way to individual university professors. Similar organizational developments have taken place in other countries in accordance with their political and cultural make-up (cf. Bernstein and Freeman, 1975). Simultaneously, public leaders, policy-makers, legislators, agency heads, and so on, have become more conscious of the availability of Evaluation Research as a tool for policy-making—increasingly, demands for evaluation are written into laws establishing programmes, and the renewal of their funding is made contingent on evaluation reports—and commentators have had reason to refer to the 'politicization' of Evaluation Research. The trend sketched above with respect to Evaluation Research is not unique to this specific activity. Similar developments are taking place with respect to policy studies, planning, organizational development, and training. Social science, purposively and specifically applied to issue areas of policy and management, has become a big enterprise. Indeed, it seems fair to state that social science, in its applied form, has recaptured some of the territory it had lost to engineering-oriented operations research and systems analysis.

From a methodological point of view, the tension between the search for precision and scientific validity on the one hand, and the constraints of political and practical demands in the problem situation on the other hand, continues. The frequent failure to demonstrate strong positive programme impacts continues to stimulate discussion. The sharp distinction between process evaluation and impact evaluation, made previously, is being blurred. It is argued that impact evaluation without knowledge of programme implementation can impair a viable programme and result in poor decisions; impact evaluation efforts may be wasteful and futile when they are based on false premises regarding programme activities. Thus, 'comprehensive' evaluation is advocated, combining the traditions of both process and impact evaluation methodologies. However, 'comprehensive' evaluation as such does not constitute a new methodology, emerging from the other two. It suggests that both process and impact evaluations should in general be conducted for an evaluation of the programme and its impact (Bernstein and Freeman, 1975; Gordon and Morse, 1975; Rossi and Wright, 1977).[3]

Contemporary Evaluation Research literature has two broad areas of concern. One is the methodology of Evaluation Research, in the broadest sense of the word, from the philosophical, epistemological, theoretical and conceptual points of view. The other area of concern relates to specific methods and techniques that are advocated and elaborated upon. The distinction between 'entrepreneurial' and 'academic' Evaluation Research, made in the context of the United States (Bernstein and Freeman, 1975), reflects the two areas of concern in practice. The distinction between 'entrepreneurial' and 'academic' involves four dimensions: (a) Relations between sponsor and investigator; (b) the nature of the researcher's affiliation; (c) values and approaches of the researcher; and (d) duration of the study.

The 'academic' mode as an ideal type is characterized by a loose relationship between sponsor and investigator, as typified by a research grant awarded by a research-oriented agency or foundation; the researcher or the research team tends to be based in a university department or school and to pursue values of knowledge acquisition, theory building and the refinement of methods and techniques; the evaluative study tends to be long-term on a relatively low budget. In contrast, the 'entrepreneurial' mode is characterized by a contractual relationship, where the sponsor needs answers to specific questions concerning policy decisions regarding a specific programme and may thus remain in close touch with the researcher in the course of the investigation; the researcher tends to be an institute or centre, university-based or not, and compatible with bureaucratic attitudes and behaviour; the evaluative study tends to consist in a straight application of available and accessible methods and techniques, to lack a theoretical framework, and to be highly structured by the administration-designed research solicitation; it tends to last less than two years in duration, but to involve relatively large budgets.[4]

The two modes sketched above blend into each other in practice. What is important in the present context is that the 'academic' mode (there are 'academics' outside the universities, too) does exist and has developed. Evaluation Research has thus been freed from an exclusively clinical perspective that tends to regard problems as discrete items separate from each other. The lack of theory means that there is no basis for comparison with past and similar programme efforts and thus no basis for the refinement and improvement of the programme; bluntly, it means that learning cannot take place. The theoretical component proposes that the social problems tackled by the programme should be 'well-grounded' in theory and that the problem situation should be subjected to a 'well-developed' methodology of evaluation. Moreover, evaluation is then also seen as a means for developing, testing or refining theories of social change, in addition to the more traditional purpose of being concerned with the effectiveness of specific programmes.

Contemporary Evaluation Research literature struggles with the problem of the definition of programme goals. The basic model assumes that goals and goal criteria can be unambiguously discovered and defined. Complaints on the part of evaluators that programme management does not clearly specify programme goals are of long standing. Thus came the evaluators' demands that they be included in the planning and design of the programme early on, in order to ensure the 'evaluability' of the programme. More recently, Evaluation Research theorists have gone beyond that. They see evaluation not only as applied social science, but as a critical aspect of the over-all political process, contributing to policy decisions and the allocation of resources (Bernstein and Freeman, 1975; Bernstein, 1978).

The problem of 'evaluability' can be, and has been, answered in different ways. 'Evaluability' refers to the relation between the problem situation contemplated by the programme and the methodological structure of evaluative inquiry. It arises because of the essentially ill-structured nature of social-problem situations. Where this is ignored, the evaluability problem becomes largely a technical administrative problem, where the vagueness of programme goals and ambiguity of expectations are deplored and attributed to the programme management and the political situation. For Evaluation Research to proceed, the evaluator will then either be satisfied with monitoring or describing the course of events and thus renounce the essence of evaluation, or he will seek to specify programme goals from the indications and hunches he may obtain, perhaps in an interactive process with programme management. Even the 'entrepreneurial' researcher is warned in textbooks and manuals that the conditions for 'evaluability' must be established and that not everything may be amenable to Evaluation Research.

Where the ill-structured nature of social problem situations is faced more directly—although it is rarely grasped in its full theoretical implications (cf. Churchman, 1968; Ackoff, 1974*a,b*; Mitroff, 1974)—reactions range from despair and cynicism (Floden and Weiner, 1978) to proposals that seek to explore, and build into the methodology, the conditions and consequences of ambiguity in the problem situation. The approach that emerges sees the evaluator interacting not only with programme management but also with other parties that may have a stake in the outcomes and effects of a programme (Rutman, 1977).[5] The task of the evaluator, then, is to define the social-problem situation of the programme and to identify values and goal images that are relevant in the situation. Specifically, the approach proposes that programme management and staff, the programme clients or target population, and the evaluators interact to produce and record programme outcomes; all of them make an investment in the outcomes and thus have a stake in the problem definition. One can even go a step further and identify population segments that are not targets of the programme specifically, yet have an interest or stake in the programme and its effects. This view places the programme and its immediate impacts in the broader context of social change and societal transformation. It explores the problem of whose goals are to be translated into goal criteria for evaluations. To consider only stated service goals of a programme as effectiveness criteria—to the extent that they are clearly stated at all—is to overlook latent goals, goal changes in the course of programme implementation, unintended consequences, and so forth. The problem is solved by including goals originating in the different population segments and groups, by identifying all possible programme effects, and by searching for factors that may influence programme effects. Programme evaluability, then, depends on the execution of these tasks (Rutman, 1977).

At this stage of development, Evaluation Research is no longer characterized by the matching of two yardsticks, viz. programme goals and programme outcomes. A theoretical framework is needed for the evaluator to anticipate salient goal values and programme impacts. In order for him to be able to apply methods and techniques to Evaluation Research, he must restructure the ill-structured problem situation without unduly reducing its complexity. This is no simple task. It is not surprising that this interactive approach has found little precipitation in 'entrepreneurial' Evaluation Research and is associated with much discomfort on the part of the administrators and politicians who sponsor and commission evaluations, and on the part of the positivistically disposed researcher. There is good reason to doubt that these newer insights have significantly affected the practice of Evaluation Research.

What Evaluation Research theory has so far been neglecting is a direct attack on the problems and dilemmas that arise and characterize Evaluation Research and are partly recognized by its practitioners and theorists. The recognition that more than one category of people will probably be interested in programme outcomes, and that therefore there will be more than one value structure and set of evaluation criteria, is a step in the right direction. But each set of values tends to be treated as a discrete item of consideration; the capacity for accounting for the configuration of a multiplicity of assumptions, values and goal images is little developed, although the methodological problem has most recently been increasingly studied in the context of evaluation research and analysis. Not only is the setting of goals and the definition of evaluation criteria essentially a political process, but the interpretation of any particular evaluation finding assumes different meanings with different stakeholders, such that the conclusions drawn from evaluation findings and their policy implications often remain ambiguous and result in a lack of utilization in policy formation and administration. Multiple perspectives need to be anticipated and incorporated into the evaluation process. Multiple perspectives enter into the conceptualization and structuring of the problem which the programme is expected to explore and 'solve',[6] and thus into the definition of programme goals.

Multiple perspectives also enter into the selection of evaluation measures and their interpretation. From the point of view of some perspectives, the wrong measures may have been selected. Having adopted a formal measurement theory, Evaluation Research tends to strive for precision in measurement and also to be concerned with questions of internal and external validity. An effort is made to overcome much of the research-utilization problem by offering a higher quality of scientific research and greater certainty of evaluation findings. Complementary alternative paradigms suggest that methodological quality in and of itself may not have much effect on the utilization of evaluative research, which depends on the 'personal factor' characterizing the potential users (Patton, 1975, 1977). The availability of better research designs, better data and better measurements is not apt to overcome the disparity of assumptions, values and goals salient in a situation; precision of measurement and concern for external validity represent but one perspective and but one aspect of the problem of evaluation. This is not to say that those concerns are not important and that Evaluation Research need not conform to some scientific ethos. But the basic issue seems to focus on the development of methodologies that are capable of accounting for the configurative complexities of programme or project situations.

The methodology of Evaluation Research is appropriate for well-structured problems. Its methods and techniques can and should be applied where the conditions of well-structuredness obtain. It has been contended in this chapter that programme or project situations are very likely ill-structured problem situations. Relative well-structuredness may be envisaged once the problem situation is understood and research questions may turn to specific, concrete items of investigation. It is at this level that the methods and techniques employed in Evaluation Research are appropriate. But given the current state of the art, they are neither intended nor sufficient to assess such problems as the significance of impacts of development projects in the broad context of social change and societal transformation.

This conclusion drawn from our review of the prevailing Evaluation Research literature appears to be confirmed by a recent critique of some forty published evaluations of development-programme projects (Bachrach, 1977). Bachrach presents a rather dismal picture of the state of the art. A brief summary of this work is pertinent in the present context.

Evaluations in the development context are still characterized by decentralization and confidentiality, both of which impair the evaluation of the evaluations, as well as the accumulation of knowledge. Bachrach concludes (p. 34):

> Evaluations have yet to demonstrate their ability to produce indispensable information on a regular basis. Aid agencies have yet to demonstrate their commitment to evaluation by including it at the stage of programme selection . . . . It is difficult to say where to break into the vicious circle of late evaluation/weak design/poor results/exclusion from programme selection and specification. It is less difficult to say what to expect from evaluation as long as the stalemate continues.

The reviewer makes the point that development programmes result from political compromise:

> Indeed, whether an evaluation can ever be better conceptualized than the programme itself is a serious question. Put differently, evaluation cannot make an experimental intervention out of a political compromise. Therefore, as long as development programmes represent political compromises, the results of evaluation will likewise be compromised.

The quotation confirms the argument put forward above: So long as Evaluation Research depends on (quasi-)experimental design and conditions of well-structured problems, the Evaluation Researcher cannot but despair. Bachrach expects evaluations to conform to the methodological tenets of Evaluation Research; yet he recognizes that the situations in which such evaluations are carried out are in conflict with the execution of Evaluation Research. He is not prepared to question the methodological tenets, but is looking for 'mutual adaptation' of politics and Evaluation Research. Evaluation Research may compromise somewhat in order to be able to respond both to the concern of politics with immediate specific answers and to the need of research for long-range, broad questions. But he also expects 'politics' to provide Evaluation Research with appropriate opportunities and circumstances.

Social-impact assessment

While the initiation of large-scale anti-poverty programmes by the Federal Government of the United States in the early 1960s provided the impetus for modern Evaluation Research, the same country's National Environmental Policy Act of 1969 appears to have given impetus to the methodology of social-impact assessment (which is referred to by its acronym SIA, undoubtedly an indication of its having 'arrived').[7] The Act of 1969 requires that any proposed resource-development activity by a Federal agency be assessed for social impact. The researchers engaged in SIA appear to belong to a different network than those associated with Evaluation Research.

The primary goal of SIA is described as facilitating decision-making by determining the full range of costs and benefits of alternative proposed courses of action; a secondary goal is said to consist in improving the design and administration of policies in order to reduce the disbenefits and to increase the benefits (Finsterbusch, 1977). Assessment is reported to include the analytical operations of research design, data collection, data analysis, interpretation, and the application of findings in policy recommendations (Finsterbusch, 1977, p. 8):

> The major problem in estimating the extent of impacts is measurement. SIAs fall heir to all the measurement problems of the social sciences generally, with the addition of having to estimate future as well as existing impacts. Improvement in the scientific quality of SIA will necessarily depend upon major improvements in measurement.

SIA authors take the reference to 'social' seriously. Olsen and Merwin (1977) are critical of the fact that past social-impact assessment has been some version of cost-benefit analysis, and argue that cost-benefit analysis is not applicable to social phenomena. They regard impacts as 'dynamic processes, not static conditions', which 'must therefore be continually measured through time'. In spite of frequent references to measurement problems by several authors, measurement theory is not one of their topics.

Most of the current authors appear to have abandoned a social-indicator methodology, which is reported to constitute one of the two major trends for SIA and is criticized for lacking a comprehensive analytical framework

(Watkins, 1977). Instead, they seem to favour some kind of a systems approach and advocate system modelling. Great efforts are made to conceptualize and diagram the linkages between inputs in the form of project action (White, 1977), purposeful action (Watkins, 1977), or values and interests, resource scarcity, policy decisions and development projects (Olsen and Merwin, 1977), and various stages of impacts. Pathways, trees and networks are drawn to show the relationships, all seemingly based on deductive logic. Watkins (1977), for instance, diagrams a structure that involves increasingly higher levels of abstraction. He begins with the 'purposeful action' of improving the availability of health facilities, which effect is measured by the spatial distribution of such facilities; together with other metrics, the state of health facilities in the community is thus assessed. An increase in health facilities brings about an increase in health-care quality, which contributes to 'collective security', which in turn favours 'mutual support', one of the 'functional pathways for goal achievement'. This corresponds to the 'actionable social goal' of maintaining security, which in turn contributes to the 'overarching social aim', namely, the promotion of general welfare. Each of the links in this chain is related to other such links or nodes of a net. What seems to be lacking is an indication of how one can go from one node to the next.

The more abstract model of Olsen and Merwin (1977) distinguishes between direct and indirect impacts. The former consist of demographic changes and economic changes, which themselves interact and bring about the indirect impacts of social structural changes, public-service alterations and social well-being. Again, there are relations between these elements. The five impacts, together with values and interests, bring about the output of collective responses, which are fed back to affect the inputs. These efforts search for ways to grasp social reality fully, yet parsimoniously.

A case-study (White, 1977) makes use of an 'impact scenario' based on a community's baseline profiles. The scenario details the consequences of project action and the consequences of the consequences over four stages. The method of scenario building is chosen to speculate on the possible consequences of a proposed project. Recognizing that the subjective nature of scenario construction has advantages (low cost) and disadvantages (the subjective construction of scenarios does not easily lend itself to predicting the magnitude or timing of impacts), the author feels that in spite of this disadvantage 'a decision-maker may utilize the scenario as a means for balancing potential social impacts with other impacts in areas'.

Social-impact assessment confirms implicitly what Evaluation Researchers have come to suspect, namely that the farther one wishes to move from the project's processes and outputs, the greater the lack of methods for achieving results that meet the rigours of scientific standards. SIA researchers do not appear to be concerned with experimental design and controls; there is barely a reference to questions of validity. They are concerned with the conceptualization of linkages and their measurements. They theorize about the relationships between ecology and social life and are conscious of dealing with communities of people, with their values, interests and goals. 'The basic operation in impact measurement is to compare the situation which will result from policy A with the situation which would result if policy A were not implemented (Finsterbusch, 1977).

Notes

1. The professional activity is here identified by capital initials, viz. Evaluation Research, while the more general intellectual activity, irrespective of its paradigmatic nature, is written in lower-case initials. In Evaluation Research literature, the word 'assessment' tends to be used to indicate the looser general process, as in subtitles of books on Evaluation Research (cf. Weiss, 1972*a*). But 'assessment' is also being formalized, as in 'social-impact assessment' and 'technology assessment'. Another word that can easily be used in this context is 'appraisal'.
2. For an account of the early history and growth of Evaluation Research, see Suchman (1967), particularly Chapter 2, 'The Growth and Current Status of Evaluation'.
3. In September 1976, Unesco's Division for Socio-Economic Analysis, in the Sector of Social Sciences and their Applications, held a symposium on 'Evaluation Methodology for Social Action Programmes and Projects' in Washington, D.C. Some of the symposium papers were subsequently published elsewhere, while others presented material that had been published already. To the extent possible, published work will be cited. Thus, the Rossi and Wright (1977) reference is based on their symposium paper of the same title (SS.76/WS/15). A symposium paper by Howard E. Freeman on 'The Present Status of Evaluation Research' (SS.76/WS/10) seems to rely heavily on Bernstein and Freeman (1975).
4. A third mode might be distinguished: 'in-house' evaluation. Here the relationship between researcher and 'sponsor' is the most intimate and hierarchical; it is therefore suspect from a research-ethos point of view. It tends to be more 'entrepreneurial' than 'academic' in its goals and procedures, but has at least the potential of a symbiotic relationship with decision-making.
5. This interactive approach is reflected in several papers contributed to the Unesco symposium (see note 3): Leonard Rutman, 'Planning Project Evaluations: A Case Study of a Bilingual Education Project', Agustin Lombana Marino, 'Evaluation of a Rural Development Project in Colombia: Critical Analysis with Methodological Conclusions'; Ilene Nagel Bernstein, 'Evaluation Research: Development and Dissemination of Evaluation Techniques'; and Linda B. Bourque, 'Determining the Worth of Evaluative Research in the United States'. See also Marcia Guttentag's essays in Guttentag and Struening (1975), and Bennett and Lumsdaine (1975).
6. Mitroff and Featheringham (1974) point to the possibility of committing a 'Type III' error, i.e. the error of asking the wrong questions when the right ones should have been asked or of solving the wrong problem when the right one should have been solved. Errors of types I and II, relating to the setting of confidence levels in the testing of hypotheses, are amply treated in statistics texts.
7. Most of the information contained in this section is taken from a recent collection of essays treating the methodology of 'social-impact assessment' (Finsterbusch and Wolf, 1977). The volume was designd as a state-of-the-art book.

3 The perspective of social-system cybernetics

An evaluation of the impacts of development projects in terms of social change and societal transformation calls for an assessment of the significance of the social change and societal transformation that may have occurred. The first chapter of this essay has indicated that such an assessment is not a straightforward task. There is no a priori clarity as to what meaning can or should be given to observed change manifestations or what kind of transformation, if any, is desirable. Criteria of significance and desirability are not given in an objective sense; they are not subject to discovery by identification in a metaphoric treasure chest filled with criteria. Rather—like ill-structured problems—they result from the interactions among different perspectives and are likely to change dynamically with time. It is therefore necessary to inquire into these societal dynamics. It is not sufficient to attempt to know these criteria at any given moment in time; one should know how the criteria come about. One must also know how change comes about; in other words, one must know how society functions and how society determines its fate, that is, how the members of a society determine their fate (under existing variable environmental conditions).

The paragraph above delineates the purpose of this chapter. It presents a conceptualization of society and a frame of inquiry for the purpose of assessing the significance of social change and societal transformation. In this sense, the scope of the chapter is limited; it is not intended to develop and present an all-encompassing model of society. Nor should the reader expect a full-fledged exposition of general systems theory, cybernetics, or social systems' cybernetics, from which bodies of thought the pertinent constructs are derived. Yet, the reader may expect to be exposed to conceptual-methodological tools with which the problem area of this essay can be entered and usefully attacked.

This chapter makes an additional contribution. The methodology (i.e. epistemology, logic, theory) employed here can—and will in the essay—be applied also to the conception of a development project and its impacts, as well as to the task of linking the latter with the context of social change and societal transformation.

Basic concepts

Society is viewed as a purposive, self-regulating, self-organizing socio-cultural system.[1] The concept or construct of system—used not as a descriptive but rather as a heuristic tool—implies that what is viewed as a system (such as 'society' in this case) is conceived and/or perceived as a whole—a whole composed of interrelated parts, exhibiting patterned inter-relationships and identifiable patterns of changing patterns of interrelationships. Like any social system, it is engaged in exchanges of matter and energy, as well as of information, with relevant parts of its environment; these exchanges take the forms of inputs and outputs, respectively. The system is disposed to reduce stress and strain by internal adjustment processes or external action. In other words, social systems have the capacity for adaptation to, or coping with, changes in their environments; the amount and quality of this capacity are important variables. Social systems are also capable of learning, i.e. of improving their performance over time. Generally speaking, the capacity for adaptation and the capacity for learning complement each other. Both learning and adaptation involve changes in the way the system's parts function and relate to each other, and they involve—at least in non-trivial cases—structural changes of some permanence.

Any part of the world can be regarded in two different but complementary ways, namely from the point of view of process (implying change and movement over time) and from the point of view of structure (implying the arrangement of matter in space at a moment in time). Thus, the geometrical figure of a circle can be described as a line whose points are equidistant from a point not on the line. But a circle can also be described as the movement of one of the legs of a compass whose angle between its legs is fixed and whose other leg is anchored in space. Both of these descriptions are valid, and each provides information different from what the other provides; they are like the two sides of a coin. Similarly, a society can be described in terms of the geographical space it occupies, of its population number, of its political organization, of its organizations and associations, of the distribution of its cities; of the amount of arable land, etc., etc. A society can also be characterized in terms of the exchanges it is engaged in with other societies, of the movements of its population and goods, of the public flows of information, of the creativity of its people, of the amount and frequency of its producing or consuming commodities, etc. etc.

Processes are carried out by structures, and structures are subject to change and movement and thus manifest processes over time. As Miller

(1978), on whose work much of the above is based, points out, this distinction between structure and process is not often made explicitly, and the two terms tend to create much confusion.[2] Any unit or entity that is initially described and perceived in structural terms can also be characterized in process terms, although our habits of perception and conception often make it difficult for us to do so. The same distinction between process and structure will be used below to characterize two sorts of system parts. But before proceeding to decompose social systems into their parts, another topic needs to be taken up.

One of the contributions of general systems theory has been to regard the world in hierarchical order from, say, the level of the atom to the level of the universe. Hierarchies of levels of analysis apply also to any societal system, which itself is embedded in higher-order systems, as pointed out at the beginning of this section. When reference is made to 'societal transformation', the level of analysis of the society is considered. Societal transformation is observed and measured in terms of attributes and properties pertaining to the society as a whole. A methodological fallacy that tends to crop up in this context is the fallacy of aggregation. For instance, gross national product is clearly an aggregated measure, but it is assumed to represent a characteristic of the system as a whole. Two countries with similar amounts of GNP, however, may exhibit quite different characteristics, depending on their respective distributions and utilizations of this wealth. Indeed, it becomes quickly apparent that it is not easy to identify properties or attributes that genuinely pertain to sociey as a whole; in this respect, the societal system is almost too big for the comfort of human experience. An alternative to the search for measures pertaining to the societal-system level would be to treat society as a 'black box' and to observe and measure its inputs and outputs in accordance with input-output models at the societal level. It is unlikely that this would be a satisfactory approach. Not only would it be virtually impossible to match inputs and outputs, but information about the complexity and the functioning of the society would be lost; consequently, the design of internal policy measures would be prevented.

The systems concept suggests that a system is made up of interrelated parts. It is thus appropriate to identify the parts of the societal system and to descend to lower levels of analysis. Society is complex enough, and our understanding of it sufficiently diffuse, to allow for many different possible conceptual organizations. In the next section, a specific taxonomy of societal system parts will be presented. Here, the discussion focuses on the basic ideas.

In accordance with the discussion of structure and process earlier in this section, two sorts of system parts are distinguished (Miller, 1978). On the one hand there are those parts that are characterized by a process—possibly a very complex process, which can in turn be further broken down—and the structures that carry out this process; and on the other hand, those parts that are characterized strictly in structural terms. The former are called 'subsystems', while the latter are named 'components'. Illustrations of the two sorts of system parts follow.

From a structural point of view, i.e. for the identification of components of a societal system, the space the society occupies can often be easily divided into regions along politico-administrative, geographical or cultural lines. The country's provinces, districts, communes or municipalities (under various names) constitute one convenient hierarchical order of societal components; although they are essentially politico-administrative units, they may display also cultural, economic and other properties that make them small societies. Each of these entities is responsible for a number of processes affecting human life. Other societal components that can be readily identified at different levels of analysis are individual human beings, various groups, organizations, associations, agencies, corporations, political parties, and the like. The government as a whole, seen as an organization, is a component of society as well. These entities are first of all identified and characterized as structures; questions as to what they are doing, what kind of processes they are engaged in, can then be asked.

In addition to human, social components, societies have also artefactual and other non-human components of some importance. Buildings, machines, the physical aspects of cities, highways, railways and the telecommunications network in its structural aspects are examples of the former. Both human and non-human components can appear as composites or collectivities, or as elementary units. Examples of the former are a group of people, an organization, and a province, and a machine park, farm implements, a herd of cattle, livestock, and a village in its structural aspects. Examples of elementary components are the individual person, a machine, a plough, and a cow. Most collective components, although essentially human, such as an organization, include lower-level non-human components as well.

However trite the statement may appear to be, it bears reiterating that human beings and groups and organizations of human beings are the essential components of society. The processes they carry out ultimately determine the character, nature and performance of any societal system, irrespective of the degree of technology a society may have achieved. This is not to deny that non-human resources may impose serious constraints on the functioning and the performance of societal systems. The significance of the emphasis on human beings as societal components will become apparent in what follows.

In contrast to the components of society, societal subsystems are more difficult to enumerate, if only because most people are not used to thinking in terms of subsystem processes. But when reference is made, for instance, to a country's education, it is a subsystem of the country (society) that is contemplated, viz. the subsystem that is characterized by the (complex) process of educating and by the components that carry out this process, such as schools and universities, the ministry of education, teachers and educational administrators, perhaps the mass media and churches. Another subsystem of society might be characterized by the process of, say, producing and marketing agricultural products; the components associated with that subsystem are farms and co-operatives of various kinds, processing facilities, marketing organizations, perhaps agricultural training institutes, and so on. When 'government' is understood as the process of governing, rather than as an organization, another subsystem is identified, which suggests that it may not only be the government that is engaged in governing. In the next section, societal subsystems will be more fully discussed.

It should be noted that in social systems a one-to-one correspondence between a subsystem and a component is highly unlikely. Rather, any one subsystem is likely to include a number of different components, and any one component is likely to engage in several subsystem processes and thus share in several subsystems. The overlapping membership of components in several subsystems is an important aspect of social systems, which will be taken up in the following section.

Before concluding this section on basic concepts, another seemingly trivial statement needs to be made: processes take place in time; they consume time. The dimension of time must enter the discussion explicitly. Certain characteristics of change have been discussed in the first chapter; they need not be repeated here. But it bears pointing out that the speed with which change and movement occur at different levels of analysis, the delay or lag of an effect taking place, and the order of events in time are attributes of processes that must not be ignored. Also, processes can be relatively reversible; i.e. the change that has occurred may be cancelled and the structure may revert to its intial state after a period of time. Processes can also be relatively irreversible; a change that has occurred may persist over a long period of time and leave relatively permanent traces in the structural arrangement.

Societal subsystems

This section seeks to make identification of the parts composing the societal system more systematic. There are good reasons for approaching this problem from the point of view of subsystems rather than components. The approach begins by identifying—and ultimately specifying—processes, appropriate to the level of analysis, that occur in the system and each of which characterizes a subsystem; then for each process the components that carry out the process, and thus share in the subsystem, can be identified. The major justification for decomposition by subsystem rather than component includes the argument that the performance of the system is of ultimate interest, and performance is a matter of process resulting from the convergence of a multiplicity of processes occurring in the system. Moreover, in accordance with the principle of equifinality, the analyst or designer ought not even to be exposed to the temptation of inferring process from structural arrangement. Also, the nature, form and make-up of components are essentially situation-specific; generic attempts at classification of structural entities have not been successful. Finally, any component, any structural entity of some complexity—and human beings are complex indeed—usually exhibits an almost infinite multiplicity of attributes and properties, such that a selection of the most 'relevant' ones must always be made for the purpose at hand. But it is the identification of the processes that the component is carrying out that provides the clues as to which properties or attributes seem relevant.

In his monumental taxonomy on 'living systems'—social and societal systems are classes of living systems—James G. Miller (1978) identifies nineteen subsystems that are critical for the proper functioning of any living system. Eight of these are grouped into subsystems that process matter and/or energy; nine subsystems are characterized by information-processing; and two of the nineteen process both matter-energy and information.[3] As was stated earlier, this paper does not aim at an all-encompassing societal model of the type, say, of Miller's effort. Rather, it addresses itself to questions of evaluation and assessment, which are essentially information-processing activities and, as such, do not involve the moving and shaping of matter-energy. For this reason, it seems justified to focus on information-processing subsystems involved in decision-making (Deutsch, 1966*a*). However, it should be fully realized that the information being processed is information about something, namely matter-energy processing structures (as well as, of course, information about information-processing). Similarly, decision-making, evaluating, planning, etc., which are processes that metabolize information, are often meaningful only in relation to the processing of matter-energy in the system or its environment.

For the purpose at hand, five information-processing subsystems can be identified and briefly described:[4]

First, the receptor subsystem. Any social system requires facilities to detect, receive and take into the system information from and about its environment. Changing the matter-energy markers that bear the information is usually necessary so that the information can be processed by the various system parts. A critical subprocess entails the decoding of the incoming information into a code current in the system.[5] The components that carry out this process and constitute the receptor subsystem include organizations and agencies specializing in this process and its subprocesses, such as an intelligence agency, an astrophysical institute or a pollution-monitoring station. Essentially, the subsystem is widely dispersed all the way to individual humans, each of whom can in principle carry out this process for the society.

Second, the channel subsystem. The information needs to be disseminated and channelled within the system among subsystems and components. Societies have entire organizations that specialize in this process, such as the postal service or the mass media. But individual persons engage in this process as well.[6]

Third, the memory subsystem. No system is able to control itself without the capacity for storing information and for releasing stored information into the decision flow. Storing is not only warehousing; it is an active process, involving breaking up 'packages' of information, recombining items of information into new packages, associating items of information with each other, abstracting, identifying and labelling information about information. Learning involves these sorts of subprocess.[7] Societies have organizations that specialize in memory processes, such as libraries and archives. But, again, this subsystem is widely dispersed; the ultimate memory processes are taking place in the minds of people. A slight extension of the concept leads to the statement that everything in a system that exists and has meaning constitutes stored information and makes up the subsystem. Structural arrangements, the channel configuration, are traces of the past and affect the way information is processed and enters the decision stream. It is the system's inner structure that determines what information is attended to in what sequence; it reflects, at the appropriate level of analysis, the values and goal images that characterize the system.

Fourth, the decider subsystem. The process of deciding is the process that reduces the variety in the information the decider subsystem receives from all other subsystems; in other words, the output of the subsystem, the decision outcome, exhibits less variety than the input. The decider subsystem directs and instructs all other subsystems of the system and can thus be considered to be the executive subsystem. However, the present approach distinguishes between 'decider' or 'deciding', and 'decision-making', about which more will be said below.The process that characterizes the decider subsystem is a rather specialized, particular process, yet complex and much more narrowly conceived than what is usually understood by deciding and decision-making. In society, the government organization is a prominent component sharing in the decider subsystem. There are others, whether formally established or not, and as will be shown, the subsystem can in theory—though rarely in practice—be dispersed over all capable members of the society. Some of these points will be taken up again and elaborated upon in the next section.

Fifth, the effector subsystem. This is the counterpart of the receptor subsystem. It establishes the output linkage with the system's environment. As in the case of the receptor, its subprocesses include the changing of the code, i.e. encoding the information to be put out into a code that is appropriate for the environmental part to which the information is addressed.[8] The components that belong to the effector subsystem are varied. Societies have organizations that specialize in the process, often the same ones that specialize in receptor processes. The subsystem is also dispersed downward to the level of the individual.

Figure 1 shows the relations among the subsystem processes in a highly abstract representation.

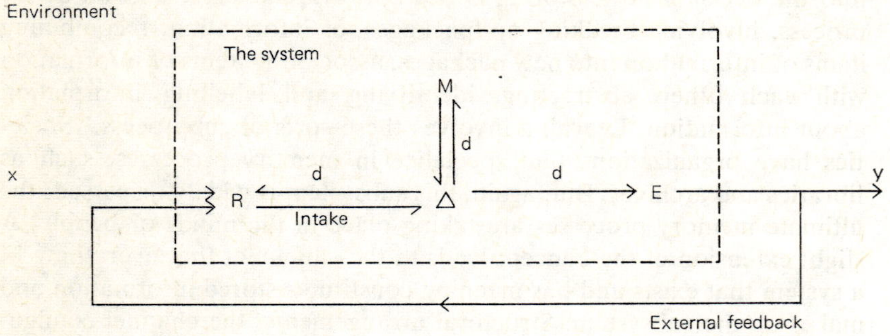

FIG. 1. The generic information-processing subsystem processes and their relations. R, receptor; M, memory; Δ, decider; E, effector; x, input; y, output; d, decision outcome. 'Channel' is not shown explicitly, but is implied by the arrows.

The reciprocal relations shown between decider and receptor and between decider and memory, as well as the external feedback loop, hint at the highly intertwined, reticular, circular nature of the phenomena represented. The gross identification and representation of the five critical generic information-processing subsystems of society can only be a beginning. It is evident that much greater specification is necessary in order to convey any semblance of real-world societies. For the moment, however, this particular topic is not pursued any further. Rather, another way of organizing society is introduced.

This second conceptual organization relies also on the concept of subsystem as defined above, namely a system part characterized by a process and the structures that carry it out. In contrast with the five critical information-processing subsystems that are generic for all living systems, the second type of subsystem asks about activities that characterize societies, and these subsystems are therefore called 'activity subsystems'.[9] The following question can then be asked: What is the nature of the generic subsystems as they pertain to any one of several activities? Care must be taken that the activity subsystems are not elevated to the level of systems, but are treated as subsystems the same as the generic subsystems. The following may illustrate the relationship between generic and activity subsystems of one society: in comparing a societal activity, such as research and development in the era of sophisticated technology, with an activity such as maintaining and disseminating folkloristic traditions in the population, it is apparent that, say, the memory processes and the structures that carry out these processes are quite different for the two activities. Thus, each of the two activity subsystems claims a piece, so to speak, of the memory subsystem. There is a chance that these two activities in the same society may not be quite independent of each other, because they may share components and subprocesses of the system's memory subsystem. This relationship between generic and activity subsystems can be diagrammed as shown in Figure 2.

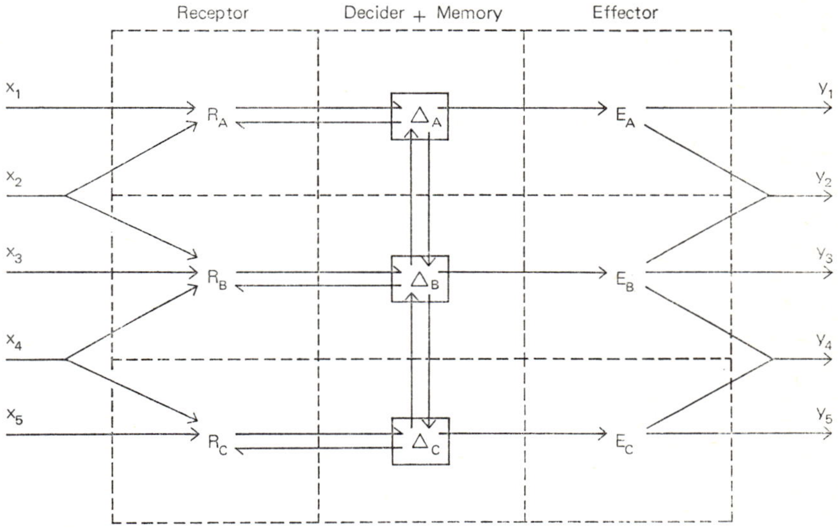

FIG. 2. Intersections of generic subsystems and three activity subsystems (A, B, C). Activity subsystems are arranged horizontally. Generic information-processing subsystems are shown in the vertical. Decider and memory subsystems are combined. External feedback loops are not shown. Multiple inputs are (x_i) and outputs (y_i).

There are many ways in which societal activities can be identified. The following seem useful and are not unconventional:

First, the political activity subsystem (polity). The political process includes the subprocesses of shaping and articulating system purposes, setting and formulating system goals, allocating resources to the system components and subsystems, directing the other activity subsystems in carrying out their processes, and seeking the attainment of system goals. The (generic) decider process is prominent in this subsystem; yet to fulfil its purposes, it requires also the capabilities and facilities of the other generic information-processing subsystems. Societies vary greatly in the organization and functioning of the polity, as well as in its effectiveness. The government organization appears as the most conspicuous component of the political subsystem; its purpose is to function as the regulator of the society. How effective it carries out this function depends on its own inner arrangements and capabilities, as well as on its relations with the other components of the political subsystem. And other components there are in any society! The polity is potentially dispersed over the entire public, which may be organized into composite components, such as political parties and interest groups of various kinds, and the members of the public may be grouped along regional, ethnic, religious, and other lines. The next section will return to and elaborate on these points.

Second, the cultural activity subsystem (culture). Following anthropologists such as Kluckhohn, culture is regarded as a process, an activity, namely the process that brings about the sharing and shaping of values, preferences, norms, habits and priorities among society's members (Deutsch, 1966*a*, 1966*b*). This view does not imply that a society's culture is homogeneous nor that there is a well-established, definite national societal culture. Rather, a society's cultural variety and the relationships among different cultural (or subcultural) groupings, as well as the impact of the cultural subsystem's diversity on the other societal subsystems, are critical variables in the understanding of any society. Among composite components in the cultural subsystem, there are religious, educational and mass-media institutions and organizations, as well as libraries, museums and the like. Most authors agree that family and peer group play crucial roles in the cultural processes. The more cohesive and integrated the cultural subsystem is, the easier are the tasks of the political subsystem. Societal instability can often be attributed to the clash between the values and norms dominant in the political subsystem and those of various population segments. Culture interacts strongly, if not, pervasively, with the other activity subsystems. Values and norms are important for the economic subsystem (gentlemen's agreement, norms of honesty); they are critical for the functioning of the educational subsystem and are, in turn, affected by educational processes. Norms, habits and practices affecting health services, family planning, recreation, and the like are thoroughly discussed in the relevant literature.

Third, the economic activity subsystem (economy). The characteristic process includes producing and distributing goods and services. The kinds of goods and services being produced and distributed furnish criteria for subdividing the economy into various sectors, each with its characteristic subprocesses and facilities. The interaction between economic and political subsystems tends to be critical. The economy provides most of the resources which the polity can allocate and, in turn, depends heavily on the polity's decision outcomes. The relationship between economy and culture has been alluded to above. As the generator of resources, all other societal activities tend to depend on the economy's performance. The interdependence, however, must be emphasized. Education provides manpower, skills and knowledge; a deficient health subsystem is likely to affect the economy negatively; family planning and population control are often regarded as economic measures; migration and settlement processes impact on the economy and are largely guided by it. Recreation processes and other processes and facilities that affect the mental state, attitudes and disposition of the population affect, directly or indirectly, economic performance.

Fourth, the educational activity subsystem. The characteristic process is doubtless complex. It implies bringing about intended changes in persons' usefully stored information patterns and heightening their capabilities for rearranging stored items of information into new patterns. Its subprocesses include learning and teaching, training and researching. The components engaged in the subsystem range from governmental organizations, regional school districts, more or less autonomous universities or university systems, to schools, parent-teacher organizations, various teacher associations, and individual teachers, students, and administrators. The structuring of the educational subsystem follows, or is believed to follow, discontinuities in the learning-teaching processes (such as primary, secondary, higher, continuing education); it can be organized according to type of education, such as academic versus vocational. In many countries, it is formally regionalized. The impact of education on all sorts of societal activities need not be detailed. In much of the literature, education is given a critical role in the development process.

Fifth, the health activity subsystem. The characteristic process includes both preventive and curative health subprocesses. The organization of the subsystem and the kinds of facilities contained in it continue to be topics of serious debate. In many countries, the subsystem exhibits pronounced differences as it affects different population segments, particularly along the rural-urban dimension. Its state is frequently considered to be an indication of a society's 'modernity'; but only relatively recently has it entered, in its own right, the discussion of the development process as such. Heavily dependent on resources from the economic subsystem and skills and knowledge from the educational subsystem, as well as on allocations by the polity, the health subsystems of but a few countries have fully gained the attention of the dominant decision-makers.

Sixth, in order not to extend the list of activity subsystems, three societal activities are considered here, namely migration, reproduction and recreation. Perhaps more than in the case of the other subsystems, these processes are carried out primarily by, and effect directly, individuals, families and households. Nevertheless, organizational components of the society participate also in these subsystems in the form of governmental and non-governmental associations and agencies. By the allocation process and by direct intervention and action, the government may have much to do with the way these processes are carried out. Important development projects may involve the resettlement of large numbers of people, which is likely to affect their participation in the cultural, economic, educational and health subsystems. Society's concern with and active intervention in human reproduction processes is a very contemporary topic and is closely linked with cultural, educational, economic and health activities. Recreation, the utilization of leisure time, may not be in the mainstream of societal concerns; but this highly dispersed and little co-ordinated subsystem seems important in the assessment of human welfare and well-being and may symbolize the little luxuries and amenities of life without which any society is the poorer.

By combining the two kinds of subsystem, the generic information-processing subsystems and the activity subsystems, guidelines for asking questions about society can be specified. For each activity subsystem and subsubsystem, questions implied in the taxonomy of generic information-processing subsystems can be asked, though this does not mean that all of the answers are readily available. For instance, at a relatively high level of analysis, we might ask how and what kind of information is taken into agricultural production from the society's environment, and compare it with the information generated by, say, the educational subsystem of the society. We may find, in a particular case, that most of the information comes from abroad and that the society itself has little to contribute. We may then want to ascertain to what extent this imported information is congruent with prevailing practices, how it is disseminated among the components engaged in agricultural production, and whether there are classes of components that are more likely to accept this information than others. We may find, say, that the average farmer is neither educationally nor culturally capable of using this information, but that big estates and industrialized farms profit from it and thus strengthen their position *vis-à-vis* the small farmers. If this happens too often, we shall then probably find an increase in tension and instability, which in turn will affect the political subsystem. Continuing this scenario, we can focus on the decider subsystem of the political activity subsystem. We may then find that previously available rules for handling such situations are no longer valid and that new rules and criteria need be established in difficult political processes. From a policy-design point of view, we may conclude that the imported information should be channelled into the educational subsystem, which may be able to process it in such a way that it can be disseminated to the agricultural production components in a form more congruent with cultural values and norms than it was originally.

At a low level of analysis, to illustrate further, we may find a village schoolteacher, an elementary component in the society's educational subsystem, who is active as a member of the local farmers' co-operative and as such plays a role in the economic subsystem of the village and, by extension, of the society. He is the only villager who subscribes to the provincial weekly newspaper, listens regularly to the radio, and receives various publications from his school district. Thus, he can also function as a component in the society's channel subsystem, bringing information about the political, cultural, economic, etc. activities of other components in the province, the country and, perhaps, the world into the village. He represents one of the links between the village and its farmers and the outside world. As a member of the board of the farmers' co-operative, he is presumably respected and trusted in the village and considered as one of 'us'; he may thus be able to play an effective role in the introduction of innovation. He may be chosen by the farmers to participate in their negotiations with the provincial authorities both to decode and encode messages between the authorities and the farmers and to share his decision-making capacity in the interest of the village. He may be in touch with like-minded colleagues in other villages, perhaps even in the provincial towns, and launch a campaign to affect the political subsystem in favour of the village population. He can do this because he has access to the societal (or, at least, provincial) channel subsystem and understands the norms and practices of the political subsystem and the governmental and political organizations. The extent to which he can afford to engage in such political activities depends in part on the constraints that his membership in the educational subsystem may entail; the school district superintendent or the education ministry may frown upon schoolteachers active in the interest of villagers, because of the former's relations with and dependence on certain components in the political subsystem.

The illustrations given above can merely sketch the spirit of this subsystem approach to system description. As illustrated, a special role in this analysis is played by the existence of joint memberships of components in more than one subsystem. A large part of the interactions or interfaces among subsystems and components takes place in the minds of people, who are carriers of information among subsystems and components and are likely to impose in the process their values, attitudes and images on the information exchanges. The next section pursues this theme further.

Decision-making: the interplay of values

As stated before, 'decision-making' is distinguished from the generic process of deciding characterizing the decider subsystem. It is broader and encompasses most of the information-processing subsystems. It could be identified as an activity that occurs in the system. Yet, it does not fit the categorization developed above. Each of the activity subsystems entails the making of decisions: there is political decision-making, cultural, economic, educational, health-care, migration, reproduction and recreation types of decision-making. But it is the configuration and convergence of all of these manifestations of decision-making that result in the system's performance and determine the nature of the system.

Decisions are outcomes of the decider process, which in turn is a function of the application of decision-rules to current information flows taken into the system by the receptor subsystem, and to information about the past released by the memory subsystem. The decision-rules that are applied at any one time are themselves effects of decision outcomes, and the repertoire of decision-rules is a part of the memory subsystem. Thus, any decision is the result of iterative interaction among decider, memory and receptor subsystems, and iterations over internal feedback loops. Decision outcomes affect the memory and receptor subsystems, as well as ultimately the effector subsystem and matter-energy processing subsystems. The word 'ultimately' used in the preceding sentence must be qualified. External feedback loops return information about the effect of system output on the environment to the system as input. Therefore, three streams of information, each one subject to feedback and iteration, are involved in the making of decision: (a) current information about the state of the environment; (b) information from the past, i.e. the system's inner structure; and (c) information about the effect of previous output. The importance of each of these information streams and their relative impacts on decision-making are variable across systems and across time for each system. Deficiencies in any one of these constitute pathologies and can be identified as such in the extreme and perhaps retroactively. But the knowledge that would make it possible to predict with any reliability and precision how much, in a particular situation, the system should rely on memory, how much on current information, and how much on feedback information, is hardly available. Nevertheless we can start asking questions. This distribution, however, is an aspect of the system's nature and character.

As stated and illustrated above, while being guided by processes, the present conceptualization stresses that processes are carried out by structures, i.e. components. Components of societal systems tend to be systems in their own right at lower levels of analysis. The relevant components of society are social systems and, in the case of individual persons, human-organism systems. They are capable of making decisions in a relatively autonomous fashion, and there is nothing inherent in human beings and human social systems that would guarantee with a high degree of probability that their respective decisions (and, therefore, actions and behaviours) are co-ordinated and integrated in such a way that a clear-cut, harmonious system output results. This is not the place to discuss why societies are possible and what makes them relatively cohesive (Deutsch, 1966*a*; Buckley, 1967). But because the subject under discussion is assessment of significance and evaluation of impacts, the interaction of different memory structures and their impact on societal decision-making must be considered. They must be considered from two points of view: from the point of view of the decision-making that occurs in a system (policy, planning, implementation), and from the point of view of identifying criteria for evaluation and assessment. In other words, both what is to be evaluated and the process of evaluation are associated with certain aspects of decision-making in the society.

It is appropriate to refer to values in the context of evaluation. The concept of value can be, and has been, characterized in many different ways. For the purpose at hand, 'a "value" is a repetitive preference for a particular class of messages or data that is to be received, transmitted, or acted upon in preference to others' (Deutsch, 1966*a*). Values represent operating rules with which information is processed. They are subject to change by internal and external feedback flows, as when a value is revised in the light of experience. They represent different levels of abstraction. In the terms of Deutsch's characterization given above, a class of messages or data may be very specific, and classes may be clustered in different ways and encompass a very broad range of messages and data. Values determine goals or, rather, the images of goals pursued in the system.

It is essentially the task of the cultural subsystem to unify and harmonize the values operating in a society. If only because of the dynamics of the processes establishing values and the differential experiences of human beings and groups of human beings, the commonness of values can never be complete across the society. While some societies may achieve a relatively high degree of commonness with respect to some values, no society can achieve the same with respect to all values. However, most societies are fortunate inasmuch as conflicting values that may be present in the society may, at the time, not be societally salient. On the other hand, events may have the effect of bringing systemically latent values to the fore and making them relevant at the level of the society, which may result in acute conflict. In the same vein, current conflicts may dissipate, not only because conflicting values are being harmonized, but also because they lose their importance at the level of the collectivity.

One of the interfaces among activity subsystems stems from the situation where a component that participates in more than one subsystem brings its values acquired through experience in one subsystem to bear on another subsystem. A farmer, for example, tends to look at the world of his experience through the screen and filter, the lens or the prism (various metaphors are applicable and in use) shaped by the values he has acquired in his 'role' as a member of the agricultural subsystem (or subsubsystem). He is likely to attend to, and interpret, information from and about other subsystems and subsubsystems and components in the light of his particular values and make decisions and act accordingly. His dissatisfaction with prices, for instance, may translate itself into his boycotting manufactured goods (from another economic subsubsystem in which he shares); his refusing to pay taxes (still another economic subsubsystem and a symbol for political activity); his more intensive participation in the political subsystem; his hostility toward perceived 'officials' of any sort, including, say, his children's teachers, which affects potentially the educational and other subsystems. Similarly, the worker who has learned to be hostile towards capital and property owners tends to manifest this hostility not only in his 'role' as worker, but also in his roles as citizen, bearer of culture to his children and peers, prominent member of a social club, and so on. A contrasting but similar case could be made out for a merchant who has learned to appreciate the values of the prevailing socio-economic order. The single farmer, worker or merchant referred to above can each be easily multiplied and grouped into like-minded segments of the population and interest groups.

Without going into the pertinent theory, it may be stated that values as characterized above are subject to change in the individual's information-processing, as well as in the collectivity. Prediction of value change is a risky matter. Single, spectacular events may bring about such change. But probably, more often, value change is due to the cumulative effect of a series of events over a period (Deutsch and Merritt, 1965, in reference to image change). The literature on persuasion contains plausible propositions concerning the conditions for such change in individuals, stressing especially the credibility of the message source and of the channel over which the messages are carried, peer pressure, and generally the context of the act of persuasion. The stability of value configurations appears to be correlated with the time in a person's life at which the values were acquired, in the sense that basic values acquired during childhood tend to be more stable than those acquired later in life. Values of collective components as reflected in their channel configurations may exhibit a similar correlation and be more stable the longer they last. It is appropriate to refer to the values of values; values are themselves valued. In formal organizations, politico-administrative entities and societies, such meta-values are reflected in constitutional provisions, ideologies and cultural-religious beliefs.

The purpose of this exposition is not to discuss value theory or even decision theory as such. Rather, it seeks to contribute to the clarification of decision-making of societal systems. If society were characterized by only one value configuration, decision-making would be simple. Everyone would see the world in similar ways, would perceive and structure problems similarly, make similar associations, obtain similar understandings and reach similar conclusions. In the extreme, it would not make much difference who was making decisions for the collectivity, except that the involvement of many would enhance the quality of decision-making because of the inevitable presence of slight variations in existing information patterns. It is clear that the situation just described is not only idealistic, but utterly unrealistic. We have at least hinted that various life situations, childhood experiences, formal and informal learning, occupational engagements, group memberships, and so on, shape people's value structures. The simultaneous memberships of persons in several subsystems and components, pointed out earlier in this chapter, explain also the difficulty of identifying any one person's value configuration—and therefore predicting a person's behaviour—on the basis of a few socio-cultural indicators. Nevertheless, the clustering of many people's individual value structures into societally relevant groupings—culture groups, interest groups—is evident at different levels of analysis and aggregation. Moreover, social interaction within groups from family to nation shape values and activate particular value configurations so that they become salient in the context of societal decision-making.

The shaping of values and the activation of value configurations for socio-cultural action on the part of people and clusters of people reflect the phenomenon of 'social mobilization' (Deutsch, 1961, 1966*b*) and the extension of the concept to broader societal processes of interest (value) articulation and aggregation. People and population segments that are exposed to new streams of information and acquire new communication capabilities tend to be 'mobilized' into new patterns of awareness, concerns, practices and modes of socialization. They may learn that conditions of life need not be the way they have been, that government is not only a matter of tax collection but also of providing services, that there are channels to decision centres that can be used and others that may have to, and can, be created, that they are members of larger socio-cultural networks and that these networks can be influenced and shaped. While this concept of 'social mobilization' covers rather fundamental processes of societal change, it is, as a concept, applicable also to micro-analytic phenomena. Highly educated and societally active persons may also acquire new kinds of information and adjust their value and behaviour patterns; university professors, for instance, are known to have acquired the values of unionization and labour-management bargaining.

In the light of the diversity of values and value structures present in any society, the question remains how societal decisions are made; more specifically, the question is how the society's decider subsystem can reduce the variety in the relevant information flows to such an extent—ideally to the variety of one—that unambiguous societal decision outcomes result in systemic action. Without discoursing in depth on political sociology and political science, several possibilities are apparent.

One set of possiblities involves various forms of power relations in the society. At one extreme, a small group or an individual may claim and assert dominance over the society and succeed in maintaining it for some time. The values of these people and of the ruling group as a whole then constitute the dominate value configuration of the society at the level of the societal system and determine societal decision-making. This situation is not much different from the situation sketched above, in which everybody holds the same or similar values. If the dominance can be effectively maintained, there will be only this one set of values that counts, and it is entirely up to the rulers to structure problems and apply their decision-rules. Dominance implies that the rulers control not only the political subsystem, which will be highly cohesive, but also that they dispose of sufficient power resources and capabilities to dominate the processes of the other activity subsystems. The larger the number of people included in the dominant group, the more the problem of value diversity is relegated to the level of the group. As is well known, closed ruling groups are likely to exhibit internal conflicts and struggles for power.

The relatively extreme nature of the sketch given above points to a number of factors that are relevant for the present discussion. To begin with, as only one set or configuration of values comes into play, the capacity of the system for information-processing may be severely limited, although decision-making may be very efficient. The system may lack the variety needed to be able to cope effectively with the variety present in the environment (Ashby, 1956). Another point relates to the question of stability. The description given above is rather static. The probability of social mobilization, as referred to earlier, taking place, the probability of people asserting their own decision-making capacity, and the probability of power resources failing cannot be disregarded. A third point, partly related to the second, raises the question of the integration of the activity subsystems with each other and, particularly, the polity's integration with the other activity subsystems. The question can also be phrased in terms of the integration and cohesiveness of the societal decider subsystem. In any somewhat complex society engaged in some development process and exposed to the vicissitudes of the international and transnational suprasystem, it is hard to imagine that economic, educational, etc. processes can in time be effectively carried out by people, groups and organizations that are not in tune with the value configuration characterizing the political subsystem, even when they do not actively oppose the dominant values and are resigned to the roles of ruled and oppressed. After all, human beings are not robots.

The usual models of societal decision-making are political models of various kinds; they seek to gauge actors' power positions, may emphasize interest groups, focus on relations among the élite or élites and general public and masses, and account for variations in countries' regimes, the political subsystem's degree of openness or closedness, and the like. Many such efforts tend—explicitly and, all too often, implicitly—to equate the political subsystem with government and to assume essentially a static, maintenance-oriented stance. Few of them explicitly deal with cultural dimensions and questions of values, dispositions and images.

More in line with the perspective of societal systems presented earlier in this essay and frequently alluded to in the course of the discussion, societal decision-making is characterized by interlocking networks and their capacities for learning and adaptation. If societal life is not exhausted in conflict among different interests or in preserving the power positions and other values of particular people, societal decision-making will be seen from the point of view of the society—and its subsystems and components—as a whole, making use of and benefiting from the capabilities of the whole. Given the complexity of society, a certain amount of division of labour seems necessary, and there will always be people who engage in decision-making processes more than others. Components tend to specialize in particular subsystem processes. Nevertheless, neither division of labour nor specialization is absolute, and the significance of simultaneous memberships in several subsystems and components has been stressed earlier in the essay. The heterogeneity of values, images and perspectives present in a society can be brought to bear on decision-making—almost irrespective of the political regime in power—if those holding positions in decision centres and specializing in decider processes are responsive to diverse views and perspectives, actively tap the available resources, seek to familiarize themselves with the current states of subsystems and components in their domains, and maintain intensive feedback throughout the society. It should be recalled in this context that decision-rules applied in the decider process are themselves results of decision outcomes. This is not the place to enter into a detailed presentation of the conditions for and the requirements of a viable societal system (Deutsch, 1966*a*). But it is necessary to return to the initial question of this chapter, namely, the identification of criteria for the assessment of social change and societal transformation.

Identification of assessment criteria

Chapter 1 of this essay reviewed theories of social change and development, which were assumed to constitute theories in use or doctrines in development policy. In the presentation of a conceptualization of societal systems, the role of values in decision-making was stressed, and decision-making was seen as an interplay of values. From this perspective, it should be clear that criteria for the assessment of what is happening with and to a society are closely related to the values that are held in the society. The thrust of the argument has been that it may not be sufficient to look to 'experts' and theorists only, but that there are probably a large number of possible sources of values and corresponding goal images.

One set of such sources is located outside the society in question. Most of the theories and doctrines reviewed in the first chapter originated in the Western, industrialized world. The principal channels for this information are national and international aid and technical-assistance agencies and their experts and consultants to governments of 'developing' countries. Another important channel most probably is higher education in its transnational manifestations. The point that needs to be made is that this information has been received and taken into the societal system and been internalized in the relevant decision-making. It is a relatively recent phenomenon that members of developing societies have contributed significantly to such international and transnational flows; yet much of the recent criticism of prevailing theories has emanated from the writings of 'Third World' citizens.

Another source of values and goal images that give rise to assessment criteria pertains to the dominant élites and interest groups, who may to different degrees be part of the international and transnational networks referred to above. The degrees of openness and cohesion vary from society to society, and homogeneity of value structure cannot be assumed. Among different élite groups within the same society, partly defined by subsystem specialization, considerable differences in value configurations may be observed. However, members of the dominant élite, the 'establishment', tend to have ways of ironing out differences, and their value differences and conflicts tend to manifest themselves at the tactical and operational levels, rather than affect the higher-order strategic and normative values.

A third cluster of value sources is dispersed over the society and finds expression in many forms. Many societies display distinct cultural differences among population segments, which reflect different value perspectives and goal images. Distinct population segments may be regionally defined; distinctions are due to geographically conditioned life-styles, such as the highlanders and the people of the plains; ethnic groupings continue to be important in many countries; some people are more 'modernized' others more 'traditional'; the urban-rural dichotomy is well recognized, as is the division into agricultural and non-agricultural occupations; many occupations entail distinct cultural differentiation. The list could be continued. The point to be made is that members of such culture groups tend to look at the world differently and to bring values and goal images to bear on societal problems of concern to them that are different from those of members of other groups. The other groups include the dominant élites, as well as members of the governmental bureaucracy.

Each of these groupings manifesting a particular value configuration is likely to establish and utilize those assessment criteria that emerge from and conform to its own value structure. Each of the value sources pertaining to the first two categories, as well as many listed or implied under the third category, tends to 'know' what is 'good' for the society and to assess social change manifestations or projections accordingly. Again, the set of criteria that will prevail or the compromises that may be possibile tend to be largely a question of the power distribution and the political struggle. What is left out is the values and goal images of those who lack power and are not quite aware of what is going on.[10] There is no need to resort to one's moral indignation or to one's own ethics. It is the societal system as a whole that is likely to suffer from the disregard of entire spectra of values and goal images.[11]

There may be little dispute with the following argument: there are many social change manifestations that involve and affect only certain people and certain population segments. It might be appropriate to pay special attention to and take particularly into account the criteria of those people who are most immediately involved in and affected by a social change. The reference in the preceding sentence to 'special attention' and 'particularly' does not mean 'exclusive attention' and 'exclusively'. Earlier in this essay reference was made to the hierarchical order of systems—'hierarchical' not in the sense of politico-administrative-organizational echelons. This comes into play here too. The village farmer cannot always be expected to consider, in the context of the societal system, a particular social change that affects him as a farmer. But he and his peers can be included in the overall decision-processes, and they may even learn that they need not always defend narrow interests. In the course of such mutual feedback relations, the bureaucrat, planner or politician may in turn learn that the same ends can be reached by different means and that it is not necessary to offend the farmers most of the time. It may not be very efficient, but most likely more effective, to attempt to identify relevant 'stakeholders' and to engage them in decision-making. The process may be quite cumbersome, but the price may be worth paying.

Notes

1. These characteristics do not necessarily define 'society'. The sentence indicates that it is considered useful for the purpose at hand to see society in terms of such properties and aspects; a different purpose may call for a different characterization of society.
2. The term 'structure' tends to create difficulty. Care must be taken to distinguish between the structure of a system, and structures in a system. The former sense refers to the spatial arrangement of and relations among the system's parts at a moment in time; usually, it is implied that these arrangements and relations are relatively persistent over time. The structures in a system are parts, entities, units defined or regarded structurally. Enumerating structures is not sufficient to characterize fully the system's structure; relatively persistent relations among the structures would also have to be considered.
3. Because, according to Einstein and modern physics, matter can be transformed into energy and energy into matter, matter-energy is used as one concept, unless their distinction is important in the discussion. The processing of information, however, involves different categories and conditions. The concept of information implies a patterning of matter-energy events, but irrespective of the specific matter-energy involved. In other words, information refers to a pattern, and not to the matter-energy that forms the pattern. While information is carried by and is manifested in matter-energy, the amount and other properties of matter-energy, beyond a minimal threshold, are insignificant in information-processing or communication.

4. The five generic information-processing subsystems treated in this essay are borrowed largely from Deutsch (1964, 1966*a*), and condense some of Miller's (1978) But neither author should be held responsible for the interpretation given here. Major deviations are indicated below.
5. Miller (1978) distinguishes between 'input transducer' and 'decoder' subsystems. Decoding may also take place 'inside' the system, that is, not only with respect to environmental information but also with respect to messages exchanged among the system's components.
6. Channels may form networks (Miller, 1978). Deutsch (1966*a*: Appendix) provides for a number of 'screens', namely screens of selective attention, of acceptable recalls (from memory), of repression from consciousness, and of acceptable and feasible policies (i.e. decision outcomes). Together they form, with the corresponding information flows, what Deutsch calls the 'will' system (or subsystem in our language). Miller (1978) distinguishes an 'internal transducer' subsystem, which enables communication among system components.
7 Miller (1978) separates 'associator' and 'memory' subsystems, which we here combine. See also Deutsch (1966*a*), particularly Chapter 8, in whose treatment various aspects of memory are prominent.
8. Miller (1978) refers to 'encoder' and 'output transducer' subsystems. As in the case of decoding, encoding may also occur between system components.
9. Economists and national planners might refer to 'sectors' in a similar sense. From the perspective of a general theory of systems or social systems, the 'activity subsystem' is not generic to systems or social systems, respectively; each type of system or social system is likely to be characterized by a relatively specific (although not unique) set of 'activities'.
10. The 'pluralist' model of the polity takes society as it manifests itself; that is, the 'pluralism' is restricted to those segments of society that dispose of the power and capacity to be 'noticed' in virtue of their active participation in the political processes. Those population segments that have neither the capacity nor the opportunity to participate are usually neglected or disregarded by the pluralist model.
11. This assertion is based on the 'law of requisite variety' (Ashby, 1956) which we interpret to imply that a complex system such as a society, embedded in today's increasingly complex environment, cannot display too much variety, as long as it can manage its own variety. Ashby's 'law' suggests that environmental variety requires a corresponding amount of variety in the system in order that the system can control itself and does not become dominated by the environment.

4 Development projects in multilevel environments

In this chapter the conceptualization of the preceding chapter is applied to project and project-impact environments. Chapter 3 depicts 'society', particularly in its decision-making aspect, as a socio-cultural system. The same conceptualization can be applied to 'project', but at a lower level of analysis. The application of the same concepts to both project and society permits the utilization of the same categories in both cases and thus facilitates the linking of different levels of analysis.[1]

Moreover, the society and its subsystems and components at various levels of analysis constitute the relevant environments of the project conceived as a low-level (microanalytic) system. Not only can they be viewed as project environments, but a hierarchical order, a layering, appears from the level of the project to the level of the society, each lower level being included in the higher level. These points are elaborated upon below.

More than in the case of society, the identification of a project *in concreto* can be ambiguous. It may be useful first to dispose of, or at least reduce, the semantic objections that the terms 'project' and 'programme' tend to create in their apposition. For some, probably most, authors, a programme consists of a number of projects; or the implementation of a programme is carried out by and through projects. (The contrary view, where a project is made up of programmes, can also be found in the literature.) However, this is of little concern here. The same phenomenon can be approached as both programme and project, depending on one's point of view and focus of attention. The development of the Guyana region in Venezuela, for instance, is meaningfully qualified by both terms (Friedman, 1969; Travieso, 1976): as a programme when it is emphasized that a number of significant tasks must be carried out in a co-ordinated way; as a project, when the regional development is seen as a total enterprise. Again, the concept of system with its different levels of analysis applies to this problem.

Nevertheless, the level of analysis at which one defines a particular project is important. The evaluation of the construction of a dam entails criteria and categories that differ from those used for the evaluation of an irrigation system, of which the dam is a part. With respect to a dam, what may be relevant is that it retains a certain amount of water within given limits, that its sluices function properly, that the calculations of water flow turn out to be correct, etc. However, it is quite clear that a dam by itself is too limited for a meaningful evaluation that seeks to go beyond questions of construction as such. Problems of construction of canals and, generally, of the distribution of water in time and space, of the resettlement of persons and villages displaced by the reservoir, of the introduction of new agricultural methods and crops, and the like must be included in the problem-setting of the effort being made to effect socio-economic change, the short-hand designation of which may be 'irrigation project'. In the perspective of this essay, the entire configuration of interventions referred to above is regarded as comprising the purpose and goals of a project. The question of the delineation of a project, that is, the construction of the project as a system, is a matter of planning and evaluation; in other words, it is not necessarily given a priori, but may evolve in the course of planning and evaluation. This topic will be taken up again in Chapter 5.

The project as an emerging system

One of the characteristics of a project is that it is created for a specific purpose. It is created, designed, planned. Even before it exists in any real sense of the word, it is present in people's minds, reflected in information flows, and affected by decision outcomes. Once a project is established and is being implemented, it has a purpose and basic goals, and the probability that its future dynamics—intended and unintended—will be largely predetermined (although not necessarily known) is high.[2] In this sense, the project is a creation of the environment or, more specifically, a creation of structures of its suprasystem. Its purpose and basic goals relate to the purpose and basic goals of the society at appropriate levels of analysis. Indeed, planning is the visualization of some goal state and of the processes that attain this goal state, and the decision to execute or implement this vision. Planning involves the designing of the basic subsystems and components of the project system; designing subsystems implies also that this mental activity called planning identifies and specifies the processes that need to be carried out in and by the project—and not only the structures that make up the project. Although these processes of visualizing and designing must continue once the project takes shape and functions, and must be largely taken over by the project itself, suprasystem planning of project subsystems and components is critical and, if well done, can save much effort, time and resources. The specification of these processes and of the structures that carry them out are necessarily situational and contextual. They are manifested in many different ways and forms, depending on the prior knowledge that is available, the certainty and confidence with which this knowledge is held, as well as the general cultural conditions and constraints. Aspects of these planning processes may themselves involve projects, such as projects to obtain information to be utilized in the overall planning process, projects to try out and refine methodologies, and the like. The Bicol River Basin Urban Functions in Rural Development Project is a project of this sort (Rondinelli, 1978). It was based on a particular theory and methodology of rural development, designed to test and refine the proposed methodology and provide the Bicol River Basin Development Program in the Philippines with information to be used in the planning process and in generating specific projects under the programme according to a new theory of urban functions and spatial dimensions in rural regional development.

Selection and design of projects often consume long periods, which in turn may affect the conditions under which the project will function. For instance, a review of eleven regional highway projects in Central America (Wynia, 1972) reveals that ten of them exceeded the 'usual time' norm of eleven months, used by the Central American Bank for Economic Integration, from the date of the bank's loan authorization to the date when construction started. The review identifies three 'decision-making points' in each of the projects that conditioned the delays: (a) ministerial decision-making (disagreements among ministers, ministerial changes), (b) legislative decision-making (parliamentary opposition that succeeded in delaying legislative ratification of loan agreements), and (c) the procurement of consultants by the national highway agencies (indecision over the selection of consultants). 'Each highway project opened new issues, required new resource allocation choices, and offered new threats as well as opportunities to highway agencies' (Wynia, 1972, p. 172). In addition, project-specific conditions for delays during the preconstruction period are reported, such as disputes between consultants and national highway administrators. While the delays reported above take the bank's loan authorization as the base line, selection and design processes precede the submission of a loan request and often involve exploratory, feasibility and location study projects. Because of the need for expertise, which often must be obtained from outside the country, political instability and presidential and ministerial successions are likely to result in a number of conflicting expert studies and designs. 'What begins as a rather simple technical decision terminates as an expensive and time-consuming policy-making morass' (Wynia, 1972, p. 173-4). Just because certain problems are perceived to be 'political', they are no less important in shaping development projects and their performance than are 'administrative' problems.

Accounts of project and programme planning and implementation cases in the development context point to the critical involvement of top-echelon decision-makers (such as presidents) in these processes (e.g. Wynia, 1972, and various contributions in Iglesias, 1976), both in a positive, supporting direction and in a negative, obstructing direction. It is evident that development planning in general and projects designed to introduce fundamental social change in particular are threatening the comfortable relationships that have characterized traditional policy-making processes and power structures. The dilemma of maintaining the old social order and simultaneously moving the country towards planned development with social equity and new forms of societal life, is a difficult one indeed.

Another environmental influence on the shaping and future functioning of development projects stems from structures outside the societal suprasystem, such as multinational and foreign financial and technical-aid agencies. Much of the development doctrine and planning and implementation methodology used in projects has originated, directly and indirectly, in such agencies. No details and illustrations of these phenomena need be given here.

What is missing in most accounts of development planning and implementation is an explicit indication of the extent and nature of the involvement of those people who are members neither of the national political establishment, nor of the national bureaucracies, nor of the international and transnational networks dominating finances and technical assistance, yet are in one way or another affected by what is going on in connection with development projects. There are failures or disappointing impacts of projects that are attributed to the fact that the ultimate users of project outputs, sometimes called clients, have not behaved the way they were expected to. Public housing projects, initially designed to provide the poorer strata of the population with decent housing, exhibited exemplary performance when measured in outputs (number of housing units) and costs, yet failed to house the poor; self-help approaches devised in the offices of financial agencies fell far short of their anticipated savings because of false expectations of what the population in question was able to do (Wynia, 1972). Schoolhouses built in villages have remained empty or are used for non-school purposes because of the particular conditions of the villages and village populations. Highways have remained underutilized because people do not need or want to go where the highways lead them. Examples such as these can easily be multiplied; they indicate that decisions affecting the project and its outputs often fail to take into account the needs and conditions of the 'clients'.

On the other hand, one could argue that the political processes, which are generally recognized to be important and critical for project planning and implementation, reflect the public's needs and demands; much of political theory makes this point. However, it appears that political processes do not always engage significant strata of the population. In terms of the taxonomy developed in Chapter 3, a large number of people are not included as members of the political subsystem of the society, particularly those people who tend to be the 'targets' of development projects and to be the most affected by project outputs.

The inclusion of ordinary people in decision-making appears, by all accounts, to have been most institutionalized in the People's Republic of China. Explicit efforts are made to elicit opinions and knowledge at the grass-roots level, i.e. in the communities and neighbourhoods, and to channel these into the highest policy-making and planning bodies over several stages; decisions are then fed back to the lower echelons for review, comments and criticism. The internal feedback loops increase the probability that unanticipated consequences, both social and physical, will be reduced; local knowledge and concerns converge in the decision-making information flows with the information patterns appropriate to larger scales and greater scope. One need not be an adherent of Marxist or Maoist ideologies to appreciate the advantages of intensive feedback and mutual responsiveness; old-fashioned democratic theory can be interpreted along these lines. Under the influence of cybernetic thinking, similar propositions have entered organization theory in capitalist countries (cf. Hage, 1974).

The project as a socio-cultural system

The project's purpose and basic goals are largely outcomes of societal components' decision-making processes and determine the specificity of the project's subsystems and components. Normally within the limits of environmental constraints they can be further developed, refined and modified, and to this extent the project has control over itself. It is probable that the project's decider-subsystem processes are partly carried out by structures in its suprasystem, particularly those processes that relate to normative and strategic orders of decision-making. The organizational relations between project and societal decision centres, typically governmental agencies, reflect the relative autonomy that the project enjoys. It is safe to say, however, that any somewhat significant development project is subject to close 'political' scrutiny and direction. Possible organizational forms range from the situation where there is a lack of any discernible project organization to one where the project is managed by an office in a ministry or a planning commission, or where some *ad hoc* interministerial co-ordinating body is set up. At the other pole of organizational form is the situation where a public corporation outside the normal governmental channels has been established specifically to achieve the project purpose and attain the project goals. The latter solution may be chosen in the case of large-scale comprehensive projects, such as regional development efforts.[3] From a structural point of view, it is often difficult to determine where a project begins and where the normal governmental apparatus ends. Although administrative and organizational theories have little predictive power concerning the relationships between structural arrangements and performance, structural aspects of the project in relation to structures in its suprasystem cannot be ignored and merit attention. Friedman (1969), for instance, summarizes the reasons that led to the establishment of the Venezuelan Corporation of Guyana by stating that the very complexity of the development programme suggested the necessity of an autonomous corporation with concentrated powers and authority, which would be capable of overcoming the inherent shortcomings of the traditional State bureaucracy. The fact that interdepartmental co-ordination had rarely worked in the experience of Venezuela, Friedmann continues, was a weighty argument in favour of setting up a centralized institution for the specific purpose of developing a particular region. This kind of solution requires a strong commitment to the contemplated project on the part of the political authorities, although they are unlikely to lose control over it.

On the other hand, the numerous instances of a close and direct connection between project and established governmental structures may reflect traditional views of public administration and political control. The frequent tie-in of a project with the president's office, i.e. under the president's personal supervision, may be motivated by the perceived importance given to the project, yet raises the question whether a president can afford in the long run to give the project sufficient attention.

The preceding paragraphs have dealt with aspects of the project's generic subsystems. Its receptor subsystem must be tuned to the information flows that emanate from decision-making components in its suprasystem, on which it depends for normative and strategic goal values. The organizational arrangements discussed above mirror the channels over which such information is currently carried. The project's memory subsystem is likely to mirror values and goal images prevalent in the relevant structures of the suprasystem. When the established bureaucracy manages the project, its norms and values dominate the project for better or for worse. As pointed out above, the establishment of a special corporation in Venezuela was, at least in part, motivated by the desire to construct the project's memory subsystem with components that were not as likely to carry the norms and values of the traditional bureaucracy. The project's decider subsystem proper, then, constitutes a lower echelon in the upwardly dispersed decider subsystem.

Like the receptor subsystem, the effector subsystem needs to be in tune with the salient structures of the suprasystem and to be connected with the latter over appropriate channels.

The project as a social system also needs to be able to process sorts of information not treated above. One sort of such information relates to administrative and technical competences available for carrying out the project. Stored information includes knowledge and skills learned by individuals in the past, as well as information available from files, libraries and archives, some of which may be outside the project in the suprasystem.

Available stored information is often shored up by including outside, frequently foreign, experts and consultants in the project; the integration of such outsiders in the project may give rise to problems. Current information flows in the form of books, periodicals and the like may increase project members' knowledge and skills, and receptor facilities for such information may be critical.

Another sort of information pattern relates the project to its target environment and other structures in the suprasystem that may be directly or indirectly affected by project outputs. Instances where project activities have faltered because of ignorance or deficient knowledge of the salient target environment are frequent enough; some of them have been referred to in preceding paragraphs and sections of this essay. The target environment may be human-social, which implies the need for attention, responsiveness and intensive feedback efforts, or non-human, which implies attention, knowledge and foresight. Housing projects have failed to fulfil their purpose because of a lack of understanding of the prospective users and because of insufficient communication with the prospective 'clients' (Wynia, 1972). Cases of ecological disasters as consequences of physical project outputs have been recorded since at least the 1960s (Farvar and Milton, 1972), many of them due to inattention and ignorance, i.e. shortcomings of the project's receptor and memory subsubsystems.

The activity subsystems cannot, by definition, be specified generically; rather their specifications depend on the type of project in question. One significant typology distinguishes between projects designed to alter the non-human environment, and projects designed to change the behaviour of people. The former include irrigation projects, hydroelectric power plants, and the like. The latter are typified by educational, training, and population-control projects, as well as projects that seek to change agricultural and similar practices. Many projects involve both human and non-human environments, and the human-social environment is never too far away even in the case of physical project outputs (as will be shown below). Each type of project implies its own specific activities and activity subsystems. There is, however, one such subsystem that is generic to all projects. It corresponds to the political-activity subsystem of the societal system, yet is more likely to be called 'management-activity subsystem' in the case of projects.[4] In recent years project management or administration has received increasing attention in the literature (cf. Iglesias, 1976).

Decision-making in the project is as much an 'interplay of values' as is decision-making in society, albeit on a smaller scale. Individual human beings with their particular values, images and dispositions consitute the project's elementary human components. To what extent they are integrated in the project system and how much cohesiveness the system displays are essentially empirical questions. Overt and hidden tensions between outside consultants and local professionals are documented, and attributed to intercultural and interprofessional difficulties, but such tensions may also arise among nationals of the same country. To some extent, at least in regard to the higher echelons, the selection of project members ensures compatibility of values in the project with values in the salient societal decision centres. Cohesion and integration, or the lack of them, in certain environmental decision structures may be reflected in the project and impede its functioning. These problems raise the question of co-ordination and control. Co-ordination and control are handled according to prevailing underlying assumptions about human behaviour and organizational dynamics, assumptions that are often not made explicitly, but follow past practice and habits. In strongly hierarchical organizations, the behaviour of organization members is 'programmed', i.e. the tasks to be executed and the ways in which they are to be executed are fully specified in advance, job descriptions are detailed, and rules are frozen into manuals. Moreover, people who do not behave the way they are expected to are threatened by sanctions which the higher echelons hold over the lower ones in the hierarchy. In contrast, another mechanism for co-ordination and control involves high feedback with socialization (Hage, 1974). The premise holds that intensive reciprocal information flows among members of the organization tune people to each other and bring about integration and cohesion, provided that there is an initial disposition toward socialization. It is unlikely that any real-world complex organization displays either one of these co-ordination and control mechanisms in its pure form. Rather, different mixes can be found. There is growing indication that faith in people is justified and that the strict hierarchical, tightly preprogrammed organization is not the best structure to bring out people's greatest capabilities (Bennis, 1966; Likert, 1967).

Before concluding this review of the project as a socio-cultural system, one set of possible members should yet be considered. Certain kinds of project seek directly to change people's behaviour and provide them with new knowledge and skills. Generally speaking, these are educational projects. A 'target population' can be identified, and the question arises whether these people should be regarded as members of the project, or rather as belonging to the project's environment. The answer to this question is important; it asks whether or not students and trainees should, at least in principle, be treated as participants in the project's decision-making processes. The question arises first from a theoretical consideration. If a 'production model' is applied to the kind of project under consideration, the target population is analogous to a block of steel that enters a factory and leaves it as a refrigerator; in other words, like the metal, students and trainees are regarded as passive objects to be processed and moulded.

On humanistic grounds, as well as on the basis of modern learning and motivation theories, a 'production model' may not be usefully applicable to the 'processing' of people. If learning, if acquiring new knowledge and skills, if changing one's habits and practices involves people not as passive vessels into which information is poured, but as participants who actively search and process information, the model will have to include such people in the system as components sharing in at least some of the activity subsystems. They then must be integrated in the project system, which may not be easy. It may not be easy because they are likely to bring into the system value structures that are different from those that dominate the project. Again, reciprocal information flows and mutual responsiveness appear as important mechanisms that need be nurtured. Recalling the problems raised in the preceding section of this chapter, it becomes clear that the functioning of the project will gain if the value structures of the 'target populations' have been taken into account in the project planning processes.

The project's impact environments

The plural form of the word 'environment' has been chosen in order to stress that there are several layers or levels of environment in which changes can meaningfully be attributed to the project in question or upon which the project has direct or indirect impacts. In the context of the present discussion, the impact environments include only structures within the boundary of the project's societal suprasystem; in other words, possible transnational impacts are not included for present purposes.

A project is designed to produce output in order to affect structures in its environment some way. It is important to distinguish clearly between 'output' and 'impact' or environmental effect. Output—or outputs, if broken down into discrete manifestations—consists of matter-energy and/or information flows. For instance, the sounds that a speaker produces with his voice apparatus, observed either as a sequence of physical events or as a sequence of symbols, constitutes his output; but the impact that he makes on his audience depends not only on his output (the speech), but also on his audience, and one and the same speech under the same conditions of delivery is likely to produce different impacts on different audiences or different people. It is the task of rhetoric specifically and of communication theory in general to find common denominators among audiences.

In an irrigation project the outputs include such things as the nature and size of a dam or dams, the properties of various installations, the size of the reservoir, the width, length and depth of canals, and so on.[5] Its impacts include various ecological changes with regard to water flow, the landscape, soil, flora and fauna, as well as human-social effects resulting from the displacement of people, the availability of water (changes in agricultural production), salinity of the soil, new diseases, etc.

The outputs of a family-planning/population-control project may be measured in the number of people availing themselves of the services offered, the number of pamphlets distributed, the frequency of relevant broadcasts, the number of contraceptive devices distributed, and the number of sterilizations performed. The desired impacts may be sought in a decline of the population growth rate or, more specifically, reductions of birth and/or fertility rates in the 'target population'. This example makes readily apparent not only that output and impact are not necessarily matters of clear-cut causality. Population growth, birth and fertility rates can be affected by numerous conditions that may be present simultaneously with project outputs. While the National Family Programme of the Republic of Korea of the 1960s is considered to have been one of the most successful of such programmes in the developing countries when measured by the achievement of output targets, an analysis estimated that it contributed only one-third to the reduction of the total fertility rate (Whang, 1976).

In the context of specifying the output, the delineation of the project again becomes important. This can be illustrated by the following example. If the project is defined as the construction of a hydroelectric plant with a 9,000-kilowatt capacity and seventy-five miles of electrical transmission lines,[6] it can be said that the project has fulfilled its purpose and attained its goals when there is no reason to doubt that the plant has a capacity of 9,000 kW and the transmission lines can distribute the generated electricity. But if we then find that the actual amount of electricity generated and distributed is far short of the plant's capacity (because of insufficient water flow), the project as defined cannot be held responsible for the shortcoming; the definition of the project did not refer to water flow, which is an environmental event. Indeed, the project's purpose and goals have been ill-defined. A more meaningful project delineation would refer to the purpose of providing the region in question, its industrial installations, etc., with sufficient electricity (as calculated on a projected need basis) throughout the year. This newly defined project would then be concerned with the construction of the plant and the transmission lines; it would also have to cope with the problems of seasonal fluctuations in the water flow and take the necessary measures, if at all feasible, to ensure an adequate supply of water to drive the turbines and enable the plant to generate the necessary amount of electricity. The goals would then be defined not in terms of plant and transmission lines, but in terms of a certain amount of electricity available in the relevant structures of the impact environment (such as factories and perhaps households). With this line of thought, impacts of project outputs could also be visualized, not only impacts resulting from the availability of electricity in the region but also impacts that might be due to such other project outputs as a large water reservoir, the leakage of high-voltage electric power into the environment, and the like. It should be clear from the previous discussion that most of the decisions relating to these matters would have to be taken during the planning stage.

Outputs are interesting only to the extent that they affect, or are expected to affect, the environment or parts of it. Significant outputs result in networks of impact that may build up to significant social change and societal transformation. The following paragraphs seek to systematize such networks. Figure 3 shows the most elementary relationship. By processing inputs (x), a project (P) functions in such a way that it produces an output (y), which effects a change in the project environment or impact area (A). Or, expressed causally, the change in A is due to the output of project P, which change in turn is caused by the way the project processes the input it receives, namely the project output. Assuming—strictly for representational purposes—linearity and additivity, the relations can be represented as follows: $dA = A^* (P^*x)$. A slight complication is shown in Figure 4, where an input into A other than project output y is added (x_A). This is doubtless a very common situation; it is this situation that so often frustrates Evaluation Research and other social-science endeavours, because the research design should 'control for' the additional effect(s), x_A, in order for the research to result in valid findings regarding the effect of y. Thus, the change in A is due to a combination of the effect of the project's output on A and the effect of some other change in A's environment, as well as to the particular properties of A. Under the same assumptions as above, $dA = A^* (x_A + P^*x)$.

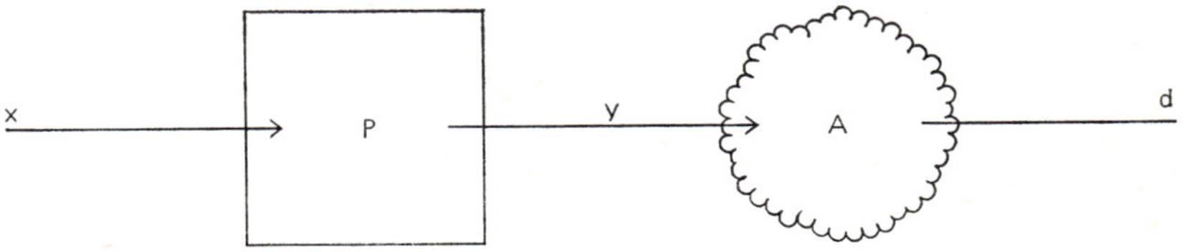

FIG. 3. Project impact.

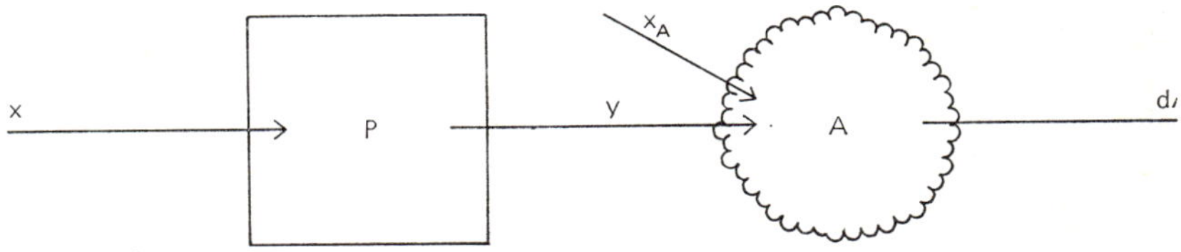

FIG. 4. Project impact. Additional environmental effects x_A impact on A.

What the diagrams do not show are the various properties of the processes and their relationships. Processes are time-dependent; that is, they take place over time. Time is variable and should be treated as a variable with respect to each of the processes of x (which is of no concern at the moment), y, x_A, and dA. In particular, the temporal relationship between project output y and its impact on A, i.e. dA, as mediated by A and x_A, is of interest. The properties of *A* are also dependent on time; structure is subject to change over time. Environmental and ecological concerns of the last ten or twenty years have alerted scientists and planners to the importance of the time dimension. When, for instance, certain methods of disposing of nuclear waste exhibit significant, and harmful, effects after only twenty, thirty or forty years, one wonders to what extent other phenomena manifest similar time lags that should be taken into account in the planning and implementation of projects. One would like to know and should know the thresholds in the size and accumulation of project output required for it to have a certain impact and 'to make a difference'. The apparent 'suddenness' of many effects is often due to the exponential behaviour of the process over time in its movement towards a critical threshold.[7] This appears to be the case with pollution. Manifestations of waterlogging, salination, laterization, diseases, etc., (cf. Farvar and Milton, 1972) tend to build up towards critical impacts such that it takes major efforts to counteract their effects. Of course, cumulative effects and thresholds operate not only in negative, harmful ways. It is generally recognized that educational and welfare-service projects, for instance, require time to mature and show tangible results, but the impatience of political decision-makers has aborted projects that were about to reach their critical thresholds. It is evident that social theory is not sufficiently capable of assessing such situations with comfortable degrees of accuracy.[8]

The discussion of project impact involves greater complexity than that implied in Figure 4. One complicating factor is the probable fact that a project has not one, but several outputs. Another complicating factor is that one and the same output may display different impacts on different environmental structures. These two situations are diagrammed in Figures 5 and 6. The probability of the presence of multiple outputs implies the probability of multiple impacts, some of which may not be anticipated. While the target output, for instance, of a hydroelectric project may consist of the generation and distribution of a certain amount of electricity and the impact is measured in increased industrial production and in the rise of certain aspects of the quality of life, the project may have to produce an artificial lake that displaces persons and villages and destroys traditional agricultural land. On the other hand, it may offer new opportunities for fisheries and tourism; the project may have given employment to numerous people and introduced them to new ways of life (regular wage income, new work habits, new skills, exposure to new population segments, etc.); it may have constructed roads where there had not been any; and so on. These are all different outputs of the same project and impact on different impact areas of the project environment. These areas may be interdependent and most likely are interdependent in some way.

The second complicating factor points also to differential impacts of one project. Yet, in this case, one and the same output brings about several effects. Each environmental structure reacts to a change in its own way

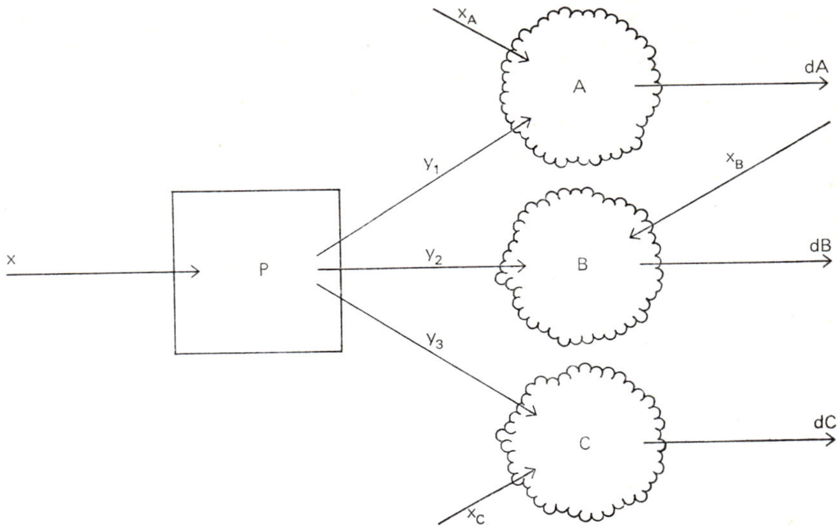

FIG. 5. Multiple project outputs and impacts; y_1, y_2, y_3 are different project outputs.

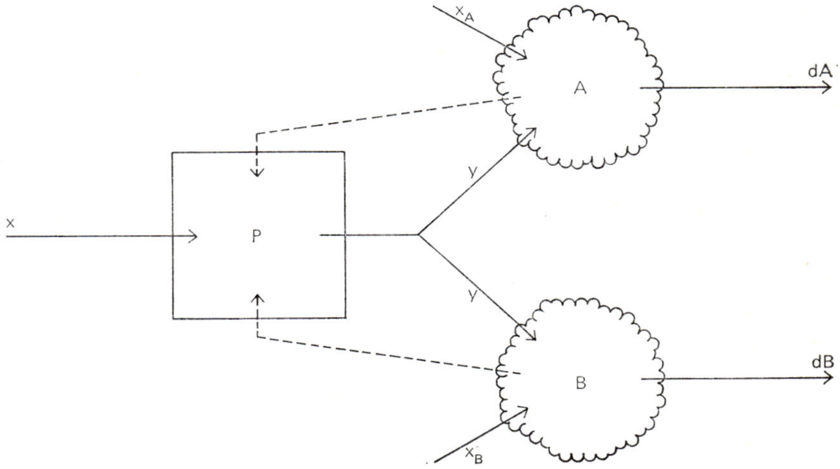

FIG. 6. Project impacts on two impact areas. One and the same project output (y) impacts on two impact areas (A and B). The arrows drawn with broken lines serve as a reminder of the necessary feedback channels.

according to how it processes the input it receives. The change in *A* depends not only on project output and other influences; it depends also on the properties of *A*. The same holds for *B* with the properties peculiar to it. To the extent that *A* and *B* differ from each other, their respective changes differ as well, in spite of the same environmental inputs to which each is subjected. For example, in the case of a welfare-service project, different population segments exposed to the same project output may display different reactions. Perhaps only one of these population segments was intended to be the 'target population'; but as it may turn out, other segments of the population were also affected by the project's output, perhaps in undesirable ways.

Things can be complicated further by recognizing both multiple outputs resulting in multiple impacts, and multiple impacts resulting from one and the same output.

So far, the impact areas have not been identified, except illustratively by examples. The immediate task at hand is to identify and organize such impact areas conceptually. The conceptualization presented in Chapter 3 is of relevance here. The societal system was decomposed into subsystems, each of which was characterized by a process and by structures that carried out the process. Moreover, subsystems and components can be further decomposed into subsubsystems, each with its characteristic subprocess, and this kind of decomposition can be carried to the nth degree into lower and lower levels of analysis. Project impact, then, is a change process that characterizes a subsystem at some level of analysis. Or, in other words, each impact area in Figures 3 through 6 belongs to, or shares in, a subsystem or subsubsystem. The word 'area' is not necessarily a spatial concept in this context. The components carrying out the change process of area *A* may, or may not, be the same as those of area *B*. In the example given above, the hydroelectric project has an effect on aspects of the economic subsystem of a region inasmuch as its electricity output stimulates industrial production, the artificial lake output affects the economic life of people, and the construction opportunities create employment and distribute wages and skills. The same project has an impact on the cultural subsystem. The availability of electricity in towns results in new patterns of living and new cultural manifestations, and the construction opportunities introduce new work habits, new knowledge and new ways of doing things. The introduction of electricity affects people's recreation and, as some studies show, their reproduction habit. A large project may introduce educational and health-care facilities and thus impact on these subsystems. Finally, without stretching the point, the political subsystem is, at least locally, affected by the project, which raises new problems, touches power relationships and introduces a new component in the political processes, viz. the project management.

At the beginning of this section, reference was made to the network of impacts. The network involves reticular relations among impact areas, which are constructed by interrelations among areas of immediate impact as

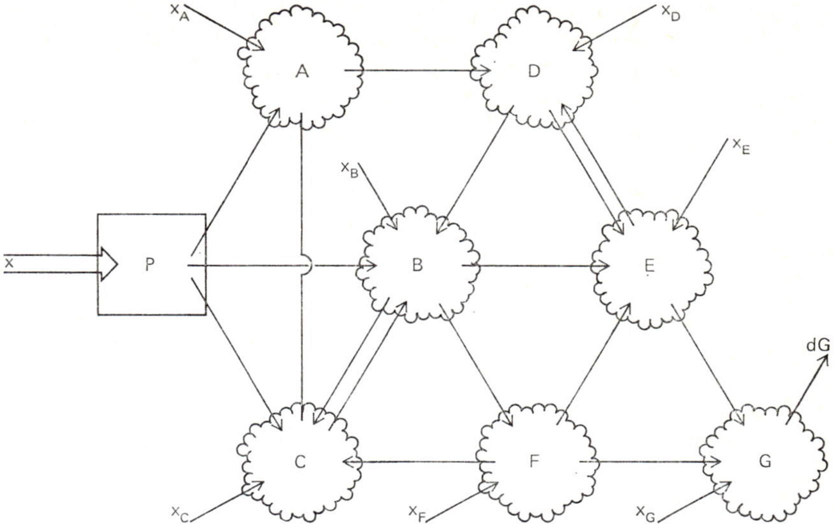

FIG. 7. A network of project impacts.

well as by impacts of impacts. In other words, a change in one area effects a change in another. Figure 7 gives a picture of a small network of immediate project impacts and impacts that are removed from the project. The arbitrarily drawn relationships can be represented in the symbols used before:

$$\begin{aligned}
dA &= A^* (x_A + P^*x + dC);\\
dB &= B^* (x_B + P^*x + dC + dD);\\
dC &= C^* (x_C + P^*x + dB + dF);\\
dD &= D^* (x_D + dA + dE);\\
dE &= E^* (x_E + dB + dD + dF);\\
dF &= F^* (x_F + dB);\\
dG &= G^* (x_G + dE + dF).
\end{aligned}$$

Again, it is stressed that the change in each area depends also on input other than project impacts or output. Circular relationships are rather ubiquitous in the real world of social phenomena; in any case, they are much more frequent and more important than traditional social science would like to have it. Loops such as *A-D-B-C-A* in the diagram of Figure 7 are highly probable, as are reciprocal relations between pairs, such as *B-C* and *D-E* in the diagram. Three of the six impact areas in the diagram receive project outputs (*A,B, C*), while three other areas (*D, E, F*) do not; but the changes in the latter can be traced back to project outputs mediated by those areas that receive direct project outputs. Thus, for example, the change in *D* can be traced back to the project via *A*, as well as via *E* and *B*. The change in *E* can be traced back to the project on the shortest path via *B* (*E-B-P*), but also through *D* via *A* and through *F* via *B*. Since both *A* and *B* are affected also by *C*, the project impact on *C* also contributes to the impacts on *D*, *E*, and *F*.

Area *G* in Figure 7 is twice removed from the project output; its shortest path to the project output includes *E* and *B* (*G-E-B-P*). It is almost outside the network and does not affect any of its members. However, it may possibly establish the linkage with another network of subsubsystems, as indicated by the arrow labeled *dG*.

The diagram of Figure 7 has been called a 'network'. In other words, it has been possible to name the whole of *A*, *B*, *C*, *D*, *E*, *F*, and *G*. It is a network and not only a set of items, because the items (the areas) are in fact (as diagrammed) interrelated; the output of any one of the areas into the network's environment reflects some contribution from each of the others, as well as from the project whose output can be considered input into the network. In other words, the diagrammed network is a system at its level of analysis. Assuming that the changes in the several areas can in fact be attributed significantly to project output and that the *x*'s with subscripts do not overwhelm the other influences, a line (boundary) can be drawn round the network system. It can be treated as a 'black box', and statements can be made about the project's impact on this system. The original network system is diagrammed as a 'black box' in Figure 8.

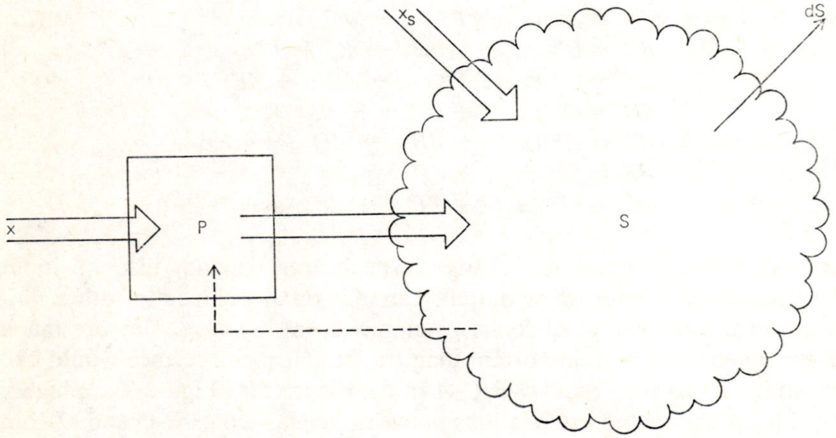

FIG. 8. The black-box system, *S*, of the original network of project impacts. In the extreme, $dS = dG$ of the diagram of Figure 7.

The statement about the project impact on the new system can be either in the form of an index derived from the changes in the several impact areas or, more appropriately, in the form of a change measured at the level of analysis of the system. In the extreme, the meaningful systemic change may be manifested in the change of one or a few impact areas, such that $dS = dG$ (Figures 7 and 8).

It is possible that a project may have impacts on two or more separate networks that are barely linked with each other or linked only at a still higher level of analysis. The illustrative hydroelectric project referred to earlier may, with its electricity output, have an impact on a region that is a considerable distance away from the site of the hydroelectric plant; but it also has an impact on the people living in the neighbourhood of the plant and/or the artificial lake. Changes in the region undergoing electrification, and changes affecting the inhabitants displaced by the artificial lake, may have nothing to do with each other. However, at a higher level of analysis, say, at the level of the societal system, political tension arising from the dissatisfaction and suffering of the lake population, due to resettlement problems and inadequate arable land, may cancel any gains derived from the electrification of the other region; political instability and violence, ultimately attributable to the project, may not allow the society to enjoy the fruits of the initial target impact. Not to overdo the pessimistic picture, it should be added that the project's artificial lake may have led to successful resettlement, increase in agricultural output, improvement of the lake people's quality of life and need satisfaction, all of which will complement the gains achieved by electrification, and the society as a whole will be better off politically, economically, culturally, etc.

The remarks of the preceding paragraph indicate that the description and representation of project impacts are not complete as yet. The impact areas have been identified as subsubsystems at a low level of analysis, organized in networks. Each network, in turn, exhibits network properties and processes such that it can be regarded as a system at a level of analysis higher than that of the initial impact areas. Relations among such network systems can then be discovered and networks of networks may be found, which constitute systems at a still higher level of analysis. The highest level of analysis considered in the present context is the society itself. Figure 9 shows a build-up of lower-level parts to systems of increasingly higher levels of analysis. The smallest circles represent the impact areas of the diagram in Figure 8, corresponding to the first, lowest level of analysis. The system, *S*, diagrammed in Figure 8, is shown together with other systems of the same level of analysis in a higher-level network. The third-level systems make up a system at the fourth level, and so on. Each higher-level system is a suprasystem of its lower-level systems, and each lower-level system is a subsystem or component of its higher-level system. What this diagram does not show is the project or the projects. They are left out in order to reduce the number

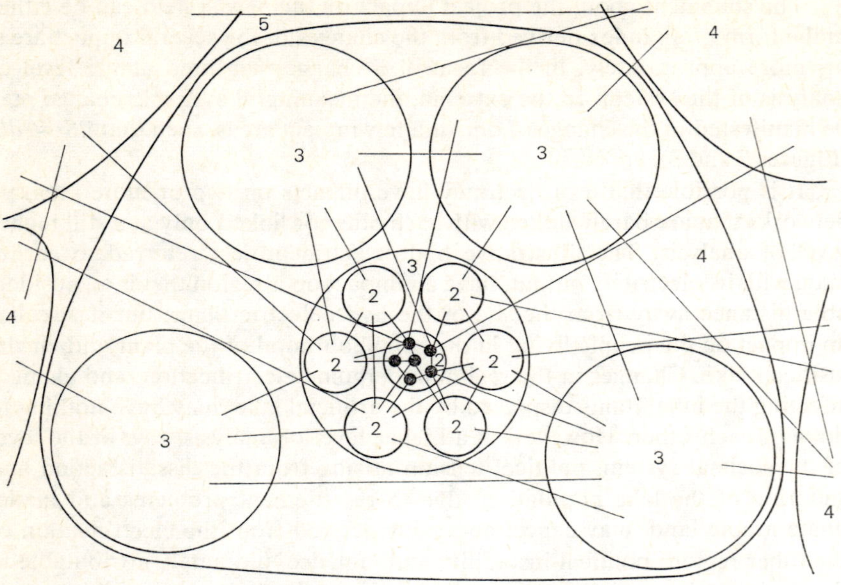

FIG. 9. Systems of networks. The Arabic numerals indicate levels of analysis. The first level, represented by black dots in one of the level-2 networks, includes the original project and the original impact areas shown in Figure 7. Level 2 corresponds to the 'S' of Figure 8. The entire diagram shows a part of a system at level 5.

of lines in the drawing. In addition to the project that produces impacts on the original impact areas, and thus on the network they form, there may be other projects in any one, several, or all of the subsystems and components. However, it need not be assumed that change can come about only because of the effects of 'projects'.

Another diagram is needed in order to show the feedback loops connecting the project with impact areas and other structures in the societal suprasystem. The multilevel steering system is diagrammed in Figure 10 in a highly simplified and abbreviated line drawing. The boxes with triangles represent decision processes that generate values and goal images and carry out co-ordinating functions. The project (*P*) carries out these processes at the lowest level of analysis.[9]

The project is responsible for managing change in the impact areas of its network. Management, i.e. steering, requires information about the state of the salient environment and its parts and about the effects of outputs. In Figure 10 information is fed back from impact areas *A, B,* and *C* to the project; the impact area *D* is 'known' to the project only through the mediation of the other impact areas. The project is thus, in principle, capable of managing and co-ordinating the four impact areas in the diagram and of effecting purposive change in its impact network, i.e. at the second level of analysis. The project's effectiveness, however, is impeded or enhanced by matter-energy or information flows to impact areas in its network from outside the network, in the same way that project impacts may be disseminated to structures in other parts of society. Other projects may, or may not, be involved. This possibility calls for co-ordination at a higher level of analysis.

As has already been stated, the project's purpose and basic goals are formed largely by societal components. A decision process at the third level of analysis sets purpose and basic goals—appropriate to its analytical level—for the subsystems and components at the second level that make up the particular third-level network, and co-ordinates their activities to bring about purposive change at the third level of analysis. Some of these second-level subsystems or components may not be steered by projects, and some—or all, in the extreme—of the third-level decision processes may be dispersed to components at the second level. In the diagram, the arrows

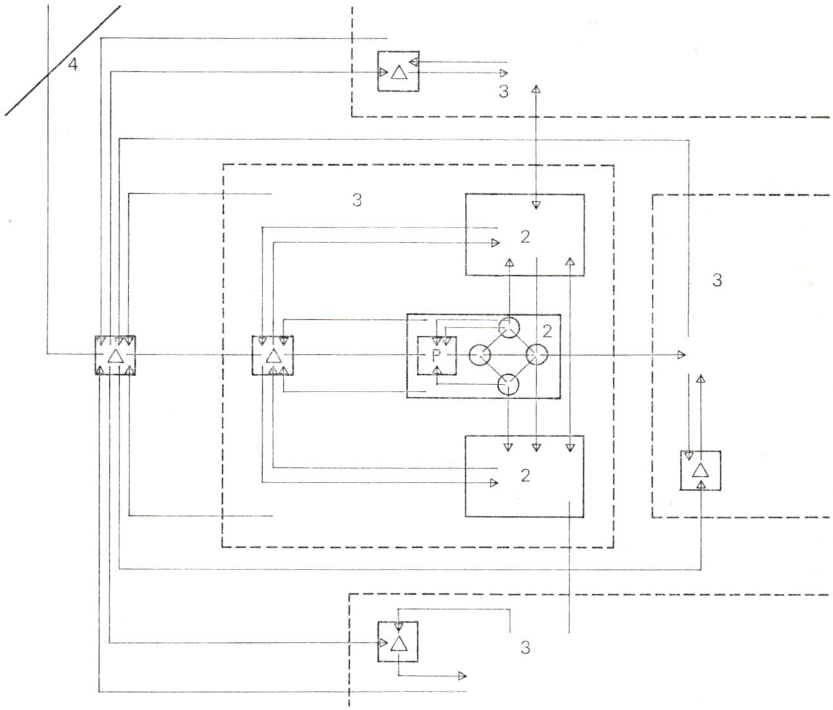

FIG. 10. A multilevel steering system. The Arabic numerals indicate the levels of analysis.

leading from the second-level boxes to the symbol for the decision process at the third level indicate the feedback loops on which the decision processes depend in order to be effective. The feedback may be discrete for any of the lower-level parts (i.e. the arrow would emanate from *A, B, C,* and/or *D,* as well as from the project and its outputs); it may be aggregated for each of the networks, and/or it may contain information about the second-level part as a whole.

Two or more third-level subsystems or components may, in turn, together compose a fourth-level part of the societal system; the society constitutes the nth level of analysis in this scheme. A fourth-level configuration is merely hinted at in the diagram of Figure 10. It exhibits its corresponding decision process, which sets purpose and goals appropriate to the fourth level and communicates these to the third-level decision processes. It, too, requires feedback information about the states of the parts making up its fourth-level network.[10] The description may go on to fifth and higher levels of analysis to encompass, ultimately, the entire societal system. The linkage with the preceding chapter is thus established. Chapter 3 proceeded from the level of the societal system and decomposed it, in principle, down to the level of the project and its impacts. The present chapter has looked at the societal system from the bottom up, so to speak, and reconstituted the societal system conceptually. It is this path that the evaluation of project impacts must take if it is to relate project impacts with societal values of social change and transformation .

Before concluding this chapter and applying this conceptualization to an evaluation methodology, a few additional points need to be made. The diagram of Figure 10 is still incomplete. The preceding diagrams show a general input into the project. This input includes not only information from decision processes in the suprasystem, but also matter-energy and other information inputs. The project depends on its societal suprasystem for resources of all kinds, including funds, as well as on knowledge and skills and personnel. Colonization and resettlement projects (or subprojects) draw people from parts of the suprasystem. Similarly, before students and trainees can become parts of a project (see the second section of this chapter), they have to be taken into the project from the environment, which usually cannot be done by force.

It might be useful to point out that the reference to decision processes and feedback loops, above, is congruent with the treatment concerning the multiplicity of relevant values and the interplay of values in decision-making (Chapter 3), a theme that will be taken up again in the next chapter.

This chapter has not gone into considerations of how the necessary knowledge might be acquired (such as empirical research) in order to be able to trace the relationships suggested by the conceptualization. Such an omission seems justified in the context of this essay because the principal purpose of the presentation has been the setting of the stage for developing an evaluation methodology in the next chapter. The task has consisted in translating the anastomatic-reticular nature of socio-cultural systems into an essentially linear language. The presentation has been couched in rather abstract terms and some amount of mental gymnastics is probably unavoidable in order to follow it. It is difficult to illustrate the arguments with concrete examples, because the concrete real world is 'noisy' and even more complex and because available descriptive theory and knowledge barely touch on such processes and relations. The next chapter makes use of and applies the conceptualizations that have been developed in this and the preceding chapters.

Notes

1. Miller (1978) refers to 'shredding out'; i.e. the subsystems of the lower level of analysis, such as 'organism', shred out to form the subsystem at a higher level, such as 'group'. The same generic subsystems, in different manifestations, are found at each level of analysis. Similarly, Beer (1972) uses the term 'recursion' to suggest that the same categories are repeated as one moves from one system level to another.
2. In the broader context of world modelling, Deutsch (1977) contrasts 'drift models' with 'steering models'. The former suggest that the given momentum carries the system processes along for a certain time span, unaffected by intervention. One of the analogies he gives is that of an ocean liner that continues to move forward for a significant distance even after all its engines are thrown into full reverse. In other words, available means of intervention cannot bring about a desired change in an ongoing process for a certain length of time, depending on the momentum and the magnitude of the intervention. This view shifts the focus from the process of intervention—it takes time for a process to have an effect—to the behaviour of the system process. That is, to use the example of the ocean liner, the more usual question about the effect of the ship's braking processes is replaced by the question about the behaviour of the ship's movement.
3. For instance, the Venezuelan Corporation of Guyana was established and given wide authority to carry out the regional development programme, although national planning, co-ordination and development agencies had existed and been engaged in similar efforts (Friedman, 1969).
4. The argument can meaningfully be made that the activity subsystems identified for the societal system recur in systems at lower levels of analysis, including the project, although the terminology may change (such as 'management' for 'political'). However, for the present purpose. no systematic taxonomy is needed.
5. From a narrowly conceived point of view, what is here considered as 'output' is effect of output, namely, effect of directed expenditure of energy, matter of information (e.g. energy expended to move rocks and soil; the pouring of cement; information that instructs villagers to evacuate the area). As stated earlier, output can be observed only as effect—effect on the environment or, directly, effect on the observer.
6. This example is freely derived from an account by Dupree (1970) concerning the Ghori hydro-electric plant in Afghanistan.
7. The analogy of the growth of a lily plant in a pond (Meadows *et al.*, 1972) is impressive: If a growing lily doubled its size (i.e. the water surface it covers) each day and, if allowed to grow unchecked, covered the entire pond in thirty days, it

might not be perceived as a threat to the pond for many days; but it would take only one day, namely, the last, thirtieth day, to increase the covered area from one half of the surface of the pond to the entire pond.

8. In the context of this essay, these and similar problems cannot be elucidated in depth and brought to some kind of resolution. They are hinted at here because they seem relevant for an evaluation research methodology, which is the subject of the next chapter.
9. As decribed in the second section of this chapter, the project itself can be further decomposed into still lower levels of analysis. In the present context, reference is made to processes, not structures. In other words, all the multilevel decision processes may, at one extreme, be carried out by one and the same person, i.e. one component; at the other extreme the decision processes may be carried out by a distinct component or set of components at each level of analysis, the components being organized in strict hierarchical echelons. The 'management cybernetics' concept of Stafford Beer (1972) is based on similar considerations. His 'viable systems' are organized in such a way that each of several decision centres makes decisions appropriate for its domain and receives the appropriate information from and about its domain; channels interconnect decision centre and interrelate lower and higher echelons.
10. It should again be recalled that the present discussion refers to processes and their interrelations, not to structural entities as such. It is the fourth-level decision process that sets purpose and basic goals for the third-level processes. This language is not concerned with the arrangement of structures or components; it does not imply a hierarchical arrangement of decision echelons, but does not exclude such an arrangement either. The decision-makers (components) engaged in decision-making at the fourth level may, or may not, be the same ones engaged in decision-making at lower levels of analysis. One and the same mind may well have to be able to think and make decisions pertaining to several levels of analysis and link the levels within itself. In a strongly participatory democratic polity, each individual must, in the extreme, be capable of thinking in terms of the group or groups to which he belongs, as well as in terms of, say, his town, his district, his province, and his state and nation; in addition, he must have the capacity of interacting with and responding to the others appropriate for each level of analysis.

5 Towards a multimethod, multilevel approach

The preceding chapters of this essay have been written with the intention of building up to, and providing the rationale for, a methodology of evaluating the impacts of development projects in the broad context of social change and societal transformation. Chapters 3 and 4, in particular, contain elements of the epistemology and logic on which the evaluative approach to be presented in this chapter is based. Before taking up the approach as such, its nature and requirements need to be discussed.

Nature and requirements of the proposed methodology

Meaningful and useful project evaluation must engage in at least three tasks. The first task is essentially descriptive; the project's functioning, outputs and impacts must be known. What is the project doing? What has it done? What are the effects of its outputs? The second task is to identify and specify the values, criteria, or standards against which the project, its output and impacts are to be judged. The third task involves comparison of the results obtained from the first and second tasks, i.e. the actual judgement. In the perspective of this essay, each of these tasks presents particular difficulties, which cannot be overcome with the traditional methods of social-science research and analysis. In order to meet the objectives proposed by this essay, the methodology must satisfy certain requirements that are derived from the conceptualizations presented in the preceding chapters. Particularly serious requirements are:

First, the methodology must take account of the reticular nature of both the project and its multilevelled environment.

Second, the methodology must consider that the situations that are subject to evaluation tend to be 'messes', i.e. that the problems characterizing the situations tend to be interdependent and that, therefore, no one problem can be taken in isolation.

Third, the methodology must cope with the 'ill-structuredness' of the situation, i.e. the multiplicity of, and uncertainty regarding, assumptions, values and goal images characterizing the situation.

These three conditions which project evaluation, as conceived here, must face, are conditions at least of high probability. It seems safe to assert that there is hardly any non-trivial evaluation situation that does not exhibit each of the three conditions to a significant degree. Traditional Evaluation Research tends either to ignore the ill-structuredness of evaluation situations or to turn such situations artificially into well-structured ones. It is disposed to attack a problem in isolation from interrelated problems, and it tends to use methods and techniques that assume essentially linear and unidirectional processes and relationships.

The literature on Evaluation Research is acutely concerned with the role of the evaluator and his relationship to the client who sponsors the evaluation. The assumption is that the evaluator who does the evaluation is distinct from the one engaged in Evaluation Research. In accordance with the conceptualization suggested in this essay, the present approach is concerned more with the process of evaluation than with the evaluator. As discussed, the process of evaluation is an integral aspect of decision-making and thus of thinking, acting and behaving. Making decisions, steering and control require the capabilities, at any level of analysis, for processing feedback information, for seeking out feedback information and for having access to feedback channels. Nevertheless, a certain degree of division of labour is necessary in complex society; specialists in Evaluation Research and analysis are needed, as are specialists in other facets of the decision-making process. The relationship between the Evaluation Research specialist and the (political) decision-maker may indeed pose problems and may require specialists in translating the language of one into the language of the other. But the problems are situation-specific and not much different from the ethical problems which today's more action-oriented science is increasingly facing. It would be unfortunate, indeed, if the dichotomy between evaluation and decision-making were maintained and strengthened at a time when a similar dichotomy of long standing—that between administration and policy-making—is slowly being overcome. Thus, except where specifically indicated, the present discussion refers not to the evaluator, but to the evaluation process and the intellectual tasks to be carried out in this process.

Questions concerning the reliability and validity of Evaluation Research findings have figured prominently in the literature, and much of Evaluation Research methodology is concerned with problems of research design and scientific methods. Indeed, if evaluation is to be utilized in the real world of decision-making involving the allocation of resources and the establishment of priorities, the findings from Evaluation Research should be valid and reliable, relationships of cause and effect[1] should be validly established, and the results should enjoy a high degree of confidence and credibility. The solution of these problems was generally believed to lie in the experimental design, which was to be at least approximated by quasi-experimental designs (Campbell and Stanley, 1963; Campbell, 1969). However, most evaluation situations of the kind considered in this essay are too complex, too ill-structured and too 'messy' to lend themselves to (quasi-) experimental design treatments. This is particularly so with respect to project evaluation beyond the project's immediate impacts. This essay proposes a change of perspective and a widening of the scope of evaluation. If evaluation is seen in the wider context of social life and decision-making and of the uncertainties and vagaries of real-world policy situations, it will be recognized that evaluation research and analysis cannot offer any greater certainty and definiteness than other aspects of decision-making, except as the process of decision-making itself seeks to achieve greater reliability and certainty. These remarks should not be taken as advocacy of, or resignation to, careless and unsystematic work. On the contrary, they imply even greater consciousness of and self-reflection on what the researcher and analyst are doing and concluding, and they imply that there is no escape into, and hiding behind, the pretensions of specific methods and techniques as such. One way of concluding this particular discussion is to state that evaluation, like all decision-making, depends on the state and quality of social theory, i.e. of the current knowledge about social processes and structures and their relationships. The extent to which a particular evaluation can contribute to the growth, reliability and validity of social theory depends on the particular situation in which it is embedded.

The following sections enter into aspects of the proposed methodology of evaluating development-project impacts on social change and societal transformation.

Identifying and specifying evaluation criteria

Throughout this essay, emphasis has been placed on the likelihood that a multiplicity of assumptions, values and goal images enter into a situation; an entire section in Chapter 3 is devoted to decision-making as an interplay of values. It will make a difference whether a project or a project impact is evaluated from one point of view or another, whether one set of criteria is applied to the research findings or another set. In Chapter 1, different theoretical perspectives of social change and development are sketched as they have been manifest over time. The kind of world view and, specifically, the kind of theory and doctrine one adheres to, determine the judgement on the significance one attributes to manifestations of social change. The same applies to lower levels of analysis and abstraction.

The thrust of the argument is that evaluation in the present context faces a number of uncertainties and ambiguities that have to be dealt with:

First, there is uncertainty as to the kind of societal transformation to which a society should aspire.

Second, given a desired societal transformation, there is uncertainty as to the social-change manifestations associated with it.

Third, given desired social change and societal transformation, there is uncertainty as to the kind of programmes and projects related to them.

Fourth, there is uncertainty as to the contribution of specific impacts to desired social change and societal transformation.

Fifth, there is uncertainty about the relationship of project output and project goals with project impact.

Sixth, there is uncertainty as to the relationship of project processes with the attainment of project goals.

The above list of uncertainties refers to criteria and standards for evaluative judgement at their respective levels of analysis and abstraction. The uncertainties arise because of the ill-structured nature of most such problem situations. In other words, different people are likely to look at the situations differently, use different theories and bring different assumptions, values and goal images to bear. Thus possible criteria and standards may conflict with each other, and there is no straightforward way to determine which are the best and the most appropriate ones. Mutual confrontation and interaction may succeed, in dialectical fashion, in resolving conflicts and finding solutions that are optimal in the given situation.

For the evaluator, it may in practice be difficult to convince his (political, managerial) sponsor that there may be other assumptions, values and goal images involved than those held by the latter. Or the evaluator may be permitted to take into account only a narrow range of possible values. The evaluator himself may not be able to step out of his own value structure, which may not bother him as long as it is reasonably congruent with that of his sponsor.

From the point of view of the evaluation process—and of decision-making in general—the determination of relevant assumptions, values and goal images at play in the situation merits consideration. At the national societal level, the political and administrative culture conditions the identification and specification of relevant values, perhaps differentiated by issue areas and activity subsystems. Evaluation at lower levels of analysis should take into account the values that entered into decision-making at the higher levels of analysis, and vice-versa. In addition, in view of long-term and time-delayed impact effects, evaluation should also attempt to identify latent values that were not activated at the time decisions were made, but that become salient at later periods of time. This identification of values acutely and latently present in the society's population is, or should be, an ongoing process, one that promotes national 'consciousness' (Deutsch, 1966*b*), i.e. enables the various parts and segments of the society to know each other, this probably being one of the necessary conditions for national integration and cohesion. Whether this is done through the country's normal political processes of parliamentary representation, referenda and plebiscites, or informally by power-holders' capacity for 'listening', or periodic surveys, or regular analysis of the mass media, or any combination of these, it is a matter of political and administrative culture and as such somewhat removed from the specific process of evaluation.

At lower levels of analysis, the identification of assumptions, values and goal images becomes more specific and technical in principle. The task consists in understanding the socio-cultural make-up of the direct and indirect impact areas of the propect. There are many ways of doing this. It may take a little imagination and an open mind to identify the people and groups of people who are likely to be acutely and potentially affected by project outputs and their consequences. Geographers suggest methods of social mapping of spatial areas. Anthropologists, sociologists and political scientists have more or less elaborate methods for taking socio-cultural inventories and identifying salient actors. Projects to introduce agricultural innovations among farmers, 'Green-revalution' projects, have failed because nobody wondered whether values held by the farmers in question might interfere with their utilization of the innovation. Accounts of sucy omissions are too numerous to be cited here

This task of identifying assumptions, values and goal images does not pose any particular methodological problems. What is important is that decision-makers, administrators and evaluators at the appropriate levels of analysis should be fully aware of the necessity of carrying out this task and do it consciously and systematically. It makes little sense at this time to raise questions of precision, reliability and validity in the technical senses of these terms.

The need for identifying multiple values applies also to the lowest level of analysis, viz. that of the project itself. Evaluation of the project's internal processes can be critical. Modern organization theory calls attention to the fact that organizations, like projects, are not machines but, in the terminology of this essay, socio-cultural systems. Thus, criteria for process evaluation should reflect the multiple perspectives represented by the members of the project. It was pointed out in Chapter 4 that social-service projects can be made to include as members those people at whom the services are directed. Their perspectives may be as critical for the functioning of the projects as are those of management and staff.

For the evaluation of project planning, decision-making and the project's internal and output processes, the identification of multiple assumptions, values and goal images and their integration is what might be called a 'meta-criterion'. Not only do multiple values provide criteria for evaluation; the question whether and to what extent decision-making processes at the several levels of analysis take into account and seek to integrate multiple assumptions, values and goal images is a criterion of evaluation.[2]

Short of developing and executing a more or less elaborate research design to identify 'stakeholders' in a situation and their values, assumptions and goal images, a more deductive research strategy might be chosen. This strategy involves the logical development of counter-assumptions and counter-values; it is an advocacy-adversary procedure (cf. Patton, 1978). The assumptions, values and goal images that dominate a decision situation can first be identified with the usual methods of interviewing the principal actors, studying documents and the like. Especially when a fairly clear-cut, perhaps extreme, perspective is found (say, dominance of economic cost-benefit thinking, the construction of a hydroelectric plant from an exclusively technical-engineering perspective, the assumption that every village needs a schoolhouse, the theory that modern medical practices are better in every respect than traditional ones, to cite a few examples), deductive reasoning can systematically develop counter-arguments and counter-perspectives that furnish a counter-set of evaluation criteria. Depending on the situation, the two polar sets can be used to develop an integrated set of criteria according to which evaluation will proceed. Or, two evaluations may be carried out, each with a different set of criteria, and the decision-makers may then be confronted with the two results. The purpose of the confrontation is to demonstrate that criteria of success and failure are not necessarily clear-cut, but may encompass a whole range of possibilities.

Each of the next sections will treat an aspect of the overall evaluation process and elaborate on some of the points made in this section.

Evaluating project planning

In the first section of Chapter 4 it was pointed out that project planning and designing may to some extent predetermine the functioning and effect of the project once it is established. From the point of view of evaluation that incorporates feedback processes and is expected to contribute meaningfully to decision-making in the course of time, the statement implies that it may be too late to evaluate the functioning project and its output and impact, except to learn lessons for future use. Thus, this approach joins the strong pleas found in Evaluation Research literature for evaluation to begin at the inception of project planning and design and for the evaluator to be involved in these processes early on.[3] Even when formal evaluation, or the evaluator, has missed the phase of planning and design, it seems advantageous and desirable to engage in retrospective evaluation, if only to clarify and gain awareness of the assumptions, values and goal images that have gone into, or have been left out of, the planning and design processes. Knowledge of the project's history provides a fuller understanding of the subsequent events regarding the project and alerts the evaluator to possible trouble-spots.

Like other sorts of decision-making, the planning and designing of projects passes through several levels of abstraction and orders of deciding. The stage for planning and designing the emergent project in question may already have been set by prior articulation of policies and programmes by the time the specific project comes into focus. Information about such normative and strategic decisions is part of the project history and needs to be known for a comprehensive appraisal.

As the prospective project takes on more specific form, the processes of project planning and design may be evaluated, rather than their outcomes. This seems appropriate because the distance between project planning and designing and meaningful outcomes tends to be great and is characterized by many intermediate stations. The project itself as the immediate outcome of planning and designing processes does not yield much information about the quality and effectiveness of the processes. Rather, it is the project impacts that count. In this perspective, the following questions are relevant:

First, how valid are the theories and assumptions that link societal values and goal images to expected project impacts?

Second, how well are these theories and assumptions spelled out, and to what extent do they enter, or have they entered, decision-making 'consciously'?

Third, how have these theories and assumptions been assembled? How comprehensive has been the search for alternatives, and how intensively have conflicting theories been confronted with each other?

Fourth, to what extent do project plan and design provide leeway for decision-making at the project level?

Fifth, how effective is the processing of feedback information for adaptability and learning during the life of the project?

The evaluation thus focuses on the extent to which the planning and designing of a project have made use of the possible variety of theories and assumptions that are relevant in a situation. The greater the variety and the more intensive the confrontation among alternatives, the higher is the probability that optimal outcomes, i.e. projects, will be obtained.

Evaluating project processes

This section deals briefly with evaluation of the project's internal processes. Although the focus of the chapter is on impact evaluation, the project's internal processes are one of the conditions for the project's ability to bring about desired impacts. The project was presented as a socio-cultural system in Chapter 4. It can be a rather complex system, with several major activity subsystems and numerous human and non-human components. It is important for an evaluative question to be asked about co-ordination of the subsystem activities and components. The only point that needs to be made here—and it has already been hinted at in Chapter 4—is that theories of management, of co-ordination and control, are many. In other words, in this context, too, multiple perspectives come into play and should be reflected in the evaluation criteria. Questions of the kind suggested at the end of the preceding section, appropriately modified, will help to guide evaluation of a project's internal processes.

Evaluation project output

Output, it is recalled, is matter-energy and/or information which the system puts out into the environment. Operational project plans and project goals are expressed in terms of expected project output, and the relationship between project output and desired impact is often implied, taken for granted, or informally established. It seems reasonable to assert that most formal evaluation research, if it is not process evaluation, focuses on output evaluation or on both process and output evaluation; the contemporary concern with impact evaluation is of relatively recent date.[4]

In the perspective of this essay, project output evaluation is evidently not sufficient—the concern is with impacts—but is nevertheless useful because it is output that has impact.

The goals and objectives that are identified as governing project output should be brought into some adversary procedure. This may already have been done in connection with process evaluation, namely, in assessing the processes that have resulted in certain goals, objectives, or targets and asking why these goals and not others. In the context of output evaluation, the basic question asked is: Why have these outputs occurred, and not others? With a view to impact evaluation, it may be particularly revealing to determine why certain outputs have not occurred, which may be a question of planning and goal-setting.

The Korean National Family Planning Programme—here looked upon as a project—established clear and definite targets of achievement, i.e. output targets. The project is considered to have been very successful in terms of its target achievements (Whang, 1976). The evaluation—focusing on programme/project implementation—does not ask about other possible outputs explicitly, outputs that may be more difficult to measure in quantitative terms. Without meaning to cast any aspersions on the Korean programme and its evaluation, and speaking strictly in illustrative terms, other outputs, such as the ways the project staff went about attracting people to the programme,[5] may be usefully identified and assessed because of their potential impacts in areas other than family planning. Ultimately, in spite of perfect target achievement, a project cannot be pronounced successful if some of its other outputs are likely to, and do, result in harmful consequences of, say, a political kind. The discussion of this example shows the close interdependence among the several aspects of evaluation, a topic that will be taken up below.

In the context of output evaluation, a particular sort of evaluation should be mentioned, viz. input-output evaluation. The evaluation criteria relate to some input-output ratio, rather than to the nature of the output. This is usually done in monetary terms to answer the question: How much input produces how much output? Theory and experience provide a standard ratio against which the actual ratio is judged. Strictly speaking, 'input-output' is not 'cost-benefit'. 'Benefit' is, or may be, more than output manifestation; it may involve some measure of output impact on the target area.

Evaluating project impact

With this section, the actual subject-matter of this essay is finally approached; but it will take still another section to actually reach it. Relying on Chapter 4, which is, in turn, largely based on Chapter 3, the focus of this section is on the impact areas and the impact network that is made up of them (see Figures 3 and 4). Several intellectual tasks are involved, each of which may face particular difficulties depending on the specific situation. The tasks are: (a) changes that have occurred—or, in the case of planning, that are expected to occur—have to be identified and specified; (b) the changes need to be related to project output; and (c) criteria for judging the changes, or lack of changes, have to be identified and specified.

The identification of changes that have occurred after the establishment or even termination of the project is a matter for social research. The research can be guided by, but should not be restricted to, the possible changes that are implied in the project plan and goals. The economy of research is also a consideration. If circumstances allow, a comprehensive, full-fledged research effort to get at all possible manifestations of change may be undertaken. However, such circumstances are rare. The strategy of research follows the probability distribution of the phenomena's relevance for the purpose at hand, from highest to lower probabilities. Of necessity, these probabilities are not statistical frequency probabilities; rather, they are based on hunches, cues and clues. The nature of the project, its plan, goals and outputs provide one set of such hunches. The more planning, goal-setting and decision-making at the various levels of analysis have taken multiple perspectives into account, the greater is the probability that the number of unanticipated change manifestations will be minimized and the range of researched change manifestations of relevance maximized. (This is one of the reasons why this chapter is organized the way it is and evaluations of project planning, processes and output are discussed first.)

The anticipation of project impacts in the planning stage poses somewhat different problems. The relatively new movement of social-impact assessment (Finsterbusch and Wolf, 1977), referred to in Chapter 2 offers methodological suggestions. Such strategies as the writing of scenarios (e.g. White, 1977) undoubtedly gain in reliability and validity when they incorporate multiple perspectives.

The second task, that of establishing causal relations between change and project output, gets to the heart of much of scientific endeavour in all areas of inquiry. Opportunities for social experimentation and for executing experimental or quasi-experimental designs are extremely limited in the world of development-project evaluation and can be found only under narrowly circumscribed conditions. Well-defined and well-structured 'pilot' projects may offer such opportunities for limited purposes. In general, however, other strategies must be chosen even if the findings appear to be less valid.

In the face of these unquestionable difficulties, the position adopted here is that a thorough, wide-ranging analysis of multiple perspectives—theoretical and experimental assumptions, values and goal images—in the several phases and levels of analysis of decision-making enables evaluative impact research and analysis to minimize the risk of drawing erroneous inferences regarding causal relations. The strategy entails, in a sense, the reversal of traditional social-science research methods. The latter tend to treat project output as the independent variable and change manifestation as the dependent one and would vary project output under controlled conditions. The configuration of multiple perspectives sensitizes the researcher/analyst to possibilities and impossibilities. If the fertility rate has declined and a family-planning project has been in progress, the temptation may be great to assert a causal relation. However, the knowledge of multiple theory and assumptions provides the first warning that other causes may be involved. Moreover, knowledge about other activities, plans and changes, derived from different levels of analysis, alerts the evaluator to the probable existence of such other causes (cf. Campbell, 1969). For example, the incidence of later marriage, the increased number of induced abortions, improvement in the population's educational level, and the like (Whang, 1976) are most likely reflected in the investigations of plans, assumptions, values and goal images at higher levels of analysis.

Still, one would like to know the impact of the family-planning project. It is not possible suddenly to stop the project in order to find out whether and how fertility rate is affected by it. (Even if it were possible, any causal inference would still be questionable.) Nor would it be possible to 'control' other suspected factors. What is possible, however, in principle, is to discover the concrete linkages between the project's outputs and the declining fertility rate, which reflects human behaviour. The research would have to be detailed, concrete, microanalytical. The population served by the project (or a sample of it) would have to be followed over a time and investigated with respect to the project outputs' effects on it. The impact of other project outputs (advertisement, announcements, etc.) on the population at large might be investigated; it might just happen that people's knowledge of the mere existence of such a project has an effect, quite irrespective of the project's target output. Alternatively or additionally, it might be simpler to focus research on events other than project output and estimate their effects on fertility rate. Also, should the evaluation of project processes show that, say, coercion and deception were used to fulfil the target goals, one may at least suspect that the project has not achieved a lasting impact and that the search for other explanations of the declining fertility rate would be in order.

In addition, other possible impacts of project outputs should be sought. Again, knowledge of the project's history, its planning and designing, its internal processes, and its multiple outputs provides appropriate clues. The notion of activity subsystems developed in Chapter 3 may usefully come into play in this context. It can serve as a guide for systematic scanning and questioning. With reference to the above illustration, it can be considered that the project in question is intended to effect a change in the reproduction subsystem; the preceding paragraph focused on this relationship. Now, it may be asked whether and to what extent the project outputs affect other activity subsystems.[6] For instance, does the way in which the project is (or has been) carried out have political consequences? If the project is identified with the State or some political authority, the use of coercion and deception, for instance, may well affect people's attitudes towards and support of the government. What is (or has been) its effect on the economy? Most activities have an impact on the economy in the contemporary world; indeed, projects are often evaluated specifically for their effects on the economy through cost-benefit analysis. Outputs of family-planning projects may easily have an impact on the health subsystem, such as when perilous methods are used, when health-care personnel and facilities become overloaded, or when certain family-planning methods turn out to improve clients' state of health and make clients better aware of health care and prevention.

The very last examples illustrate the possibility that the effectiveness (and cost-benefit ratio) of many projects may be enhanced when a project is designed to affect more than one activity subsystem and has multiple, inter-related goals.[7]

This configurative strategy does not replace (quasi-) experimental design methods where such methods are feasible. It embodies the conceptualization presented in the third and fourth chapters. Because the strategy cannot be demonstrated except by carrying it out in the real world of development projects, it was thought useful to treat the conceptualization in great detail. If Chapters 3 and 4 are properly assimilated, the reader will be able to give this research strategy at least a reasonable degree of plausibility.

As to the third task in impact evaluation, the task of identifying and specifying evaluation criteria, there is no need to go much beyond what has been said already in this chapter. The analysis and integration of multiple perspectives is again the key. These perspectives are found not only in the theories and doctrines that guide the project, they are found not only in the project's leadership and among its decision-makers: they are found also in the population actually and potentially affected by project output. It should be noted that information about these multiple perspectives is needed also for carrying out the second task as discussed above.

Evaluating impacts of impacts

Given the purpose of this essay, evaluations of project planning, project process, project output and project impact are auxiliary to the evaluation of a project's contributions to social change and societal transformation. They are auxiliary in the sense that the information they generate helps to understand change events at higher levels of analysis and to link them to the level of the project. Yet they do not tell us anything about the relation between project on the one hand and higher-order social change and societal transformation on the other—unless the theories we hold and the assumptions we are prepared to make established this relationship. Earlier parts of this essay have argued that such theories and assumptions are uncertain at best and that there has been a multiplicity of theories and doctrines that have guided development policies and strategies.

The task of this section is to trace conceptually the paths through which immediate project impacts are diffused through the system and effect change in other areas and at higher levels of analysis, and to discuss the identification of evaluation criteria. Reference is made to the diagram of Figure 10, which represents a multilevel steering system. As the impact moves away from the project and its immediate impact, causal relationships become more and more vague, and the effect of project output threatens to vanish.

The first step in the evaluation of impacts of impacts consists in identifying and specifying further changes that result from project impact. If there is not any further impact, whatever social change that may have occurred as a consequence of project output will remain limited, and no transformation will take place. One reservation, however, needs to be made, viz. further effects of project impact may be delayed in time, a factor that must be taken into account.

If people do not make use, or have no opportunity to make use, of their newly gained literacy skills and are not otherwise affected by them, nothing more is going to happen, and the literacy project may as well not have taken place (although the increase in literacy rate will show in statistics). In contrast, when literacy leads to, say, higher productivity and greater political awareness, social change can be said to have occurred, and societal transformation seems possible. However, in some people's views, greater political awareness may be undesirable because of its possible consequences, while higher productivity is welcome; others may place a higher value on political awareness and consider the increase in productivity less important. This illustrates a case of two different perspectives, each of which makes certain assumptions about the desirability of a possible expected societal transformation and about the desirability of a change that has occurred.

The identification of impacts and further impacts follows a strategy similar to the one presented in the preceding section regarding the search for project impacts. The search for further impacts must take into account the fact that the path of the diffusion of effects is not necessarily linear and unidirectional; rather, there is a high probability that it will be circular and include events that affect each other. A revealing test seeks to establish whether impact loops are negative or positive. A negative loop contains at least one, or an odd number of, negative relations between pairs of events,[8] while a positive loop has no, or an even number of, positive relations (Maruyama, 1963). Positive loops of effects tend to be self-reinforcing; in other words, without intervention of exogenous variables, they tend to amplify the deviation from an initial state and threaten eventually to 'explode' (cf. Rastogi, 1977 for a dynamic societal model consisting of six positive loops). Negative loops tend to have a dampening effect on change. Morphogenesis, i.e. the formation of new structures, results from self-reinforcing deviation-amplifying mutual causal relationships (Maruyama, 1963; Buckley, 1967) and is a prerequisite for societal transformation. Evaluation may search for such conditions in order to appraise the likelihood of what, if anything, may be happening to the system.

It is clear that the question can no longer be that of the effect of a specific project. Rather, configurations of projects and non-project events are what are important. This raises new questions, which have rarely been asked in the literature and for which there are hardly any answers: Does it make a difference how events are patterned in such configurations? Is a certain sequence of events (impacts) more effective than another sequence of the same events? Can impact events wait for each other as they are needed to constitute a configuration? Answers to such (unasked) questions are often implicitly assumed in theories and doctrines of development.

The identification of evaluation criteria at the different levels of the impact nets does not pose any new problems. Increasingly as higher levels of analysis are reached, the criteria derive from conceptions of desirable societal transformation and from expectations of the relationship between change manifestations and a desired transformation. In order to identify some 'optimal' criterion, the dialectic method of confronting conflicting theories and assumptions is appropriate; assumptions must be made explicit and theories have to be searched for. In addition, however, at each level of analysis, impacts should also be evaluated against criteria generated with respect to a more immediate effect of the change, rather than only with respect to higher-order change effects on the values of societal transformation. The focus on the more immediate change effects increases the probability that people and conditions in the impact area are taken into account in the generation of evaluation criteria. Thus two (or more) sets of evaluation criteria may be generated, which implies that two (or more) different evaluations may be conducted. The first evaluation seeks to relate observed change effects to visions of desired societal transformation; it assumes a wide time horizon and contemplates the fate of society as a whole. The second evaluation assumes a shorter time horizon and is concerned with the effect of observed change events on parts of the system. (There may be more than two such evaluations because the categories of classification are relative. In other words, there may be several meaningful time horizons and several conceptions of system parts relevant in the situation that is considered.) We are dealing here with situations that are familiar to social philosophers: short-term benefits versus long-term costs, or vice-versa; conflict between the collective interests and particular interests. Societies must face 'tragic choices' (Calabresi and Bobbitt, 1978). Evaluation does not resolve such conflicts and dilemmas. But the conscious search for and application of evaluation criteria makes such tensions explicit and may lead to constructive confrontation.

Chapter summary and synthesis

The several sections of this chapter need to be brought together and synthesized. They have been written in a quasi-analytical mode; that is, the intricate network of the intellectual activities of concern has been pulled apart and each major segment has been treated separately.

In order to facilitate the task, we shall resort to the device of describing the manifold of evaluation processes as if they were carried out by a single super-mind. We call this being 'the Evaluator' although, as will be seen, the name does not convey all there is. The Evaluator is fictitious; he is an artificial device for the convenience of presentation and representation.

The purpose of the Evaluator is to assess the possible and potential contributions that specific development projects may make to a given society's transformation. Should the Evaluator find that a project does not yield any result in terms of desirable transformation or that it pushes the society in an undesirable direction, the project can be terminated or modified, or counter-projects may have to be developed. In the case of positive findings, the project can be reinforced and supplemented. Moreover, evaluation findings along the network constituted by the several phases presented in the preceding sections of this chapter may furnish information that can be utilized in the ongoing societal steering process (formative evaluation).

The Evaluator's first task is to gather and process information, to understand the society in question and to have a good grasp of the basic values and goal images that are present in the society. The second task is to identify theories and doctrines that are used in the formation of the society's development policies and strategies, as well as those theories and doctrines that may not be manifest in actual policy formation but are nevertheless plausible. A first evaluation occurs at this stage: The Evaluator should be able to assess the congruence of societal values and goal images with the theories and doctrines. The information from the first and second tasks and the initial evaluation will be used later on in the evaluation network. A lack of congruence predicts trouble spots in policy, programme and project implementation. The execution of these tasks will provide the Evaluator with a frame of reference which he (the Evaluator) will use in evaluating project impacts and impacts of impacts.

If the notion of the Evaluator is abandoned for a moment and the government is envisioned, the above tasks call for a comprehensive information system that allows the government and the society at large to collect, process and have accessible the necessary and appropriate information. It also requires open minds on the part of those responsible for the designing, implementing and using of such an information system, which would be a project in and by itself. This is not the place to elaborate on such a project. It must suffice to point out that even under present circumstances and without sophisticated technology, governments can achieve much along these lines.

The next task of the Evaluator is to focus on the processes of planning and designing the project. This may be done after the fact; ideally, it should be done while these processes are under way. The third section of this chapter treats this phase. The Evaluator asks about the degree of congruence between project formation and the underlying theories and doctrines. Questions need to be asked about the degree to which conflicting assumptions, values and goal images have entered the decision-making of project planning and designing. Of particular interest are the purpose and goal that are given to the emergent project. How do they relate to basic assumptions, values and goal images in the society and, particularly, among those who are affected the most immediately by expected project outputs? Information from the first and second tasks may help to balance particularistic and universal concerns. This last sentence points to one of the many incidents where policy/programme/project formation merges with evaluation; the balancing of universal (i.e. societal) concerns and particularistic concerns should be part of the former activity, yet benefits from evaluative outcomes.

In carrying out the above and subsequent tasks, the Evaluator will usefully resort to the decomposition of social systems into generic and activity subsystems (see Chapter 3), an organizing scheme that may also be underlying policy/planning activities. The present text would be too much burdened if the scheme were systematically explored. The reader is invited to consider the Evaluator's questions, for instance, about the way information is received for the planning activities, whether information about the educational subsystem is readily available, whether the deciding processes for project planning are biased because information about the health-activity subsystem is lacking, and so on for other generic and activity subsystems.

The fourth task of the Evaluator is to focus on the project's processes and outputs; the fourth and fifth sections of this chapter discuss this aspect. In larger-scale, ongoing development efforts, information generated by the execution of this task can be fed back to project planning/designing processes and may affect theory and doctrine. The way this feedback information is processed becomes then an additional criterion for evaluating planning and designing.

Having stored the information generated by the first four tasks for subsequent use and, as appropriate, having released it into the decision-making processes, the Evaluator directs his attention to project impacts (see the sixth section above). Not only do anticipated and unanticipated impacts need to be identified and linked to project outputs; the Evaluator will identify the values, assumptions and goal images present in the impact areas. To evaluate the impacts, a wide range of possible assumptions, values and goal images is needed; the execution of the previous task should have provided much of the relevant information, and information about the impact areas is derived from the latter. The Evaluator himself has to process feedback information and be guided by its previous output effects in carrying out its processes. In focusing on the level of impact areas, the Evaluator may find that his identification of societal values, assumptions, goal images, theories and doctrines has been, say, too general and abstract, or too one-sided. At the concrete level of impact areas, views that had no opportunity to manifest themselves at the higher levels of analysis may be tapped and brought into the larger picture.

The Evaluator is interested in the degree to which the decision-areas at the various levels of analysis (see Figure 10) are sensitive to evaluative findings regarding project impacts. In a dynamic situation, values, assumptions, goal images are affected by knowledge about concrete change effected by concrete events. It need hardly be mentioned that evaluative information about project impact needs to be fed back to and processed by the project and the structures that control it.

The Evaluator then searches for impacts of impacts (or second, third, etc. orders of change), for values affected by such changes, for theories that claim to link change events within and across change orders and levels of analysis. The question of fundamental social change and societal transformation becomes increasingly acute as the investigation moves away from project output and immediate impact. The Evaluator must take into account a multiplicity of factors (including other project outputs) that may have something to do with the observed change. Increasingly, the evaluation affects not so much the performance of the original project, but rather governmental and societal policy and its underlying theories and doctrines.

Changes in the latter will or should affect the original project in continuous iterative cycles. It is the Evaluator who generates the information that steers formation and implementation of decision-making from the policy level to the project level and back again. Evaluation, thus, becomes part of the decision-making processes; it can no longer be isolated as an activity in and by itself.

Turning to societal transformation, the Evaluator will assess the degree to which changes that have occurred are relatively persistent and involve changes in structure. Here he must resort to available theory—and perhaps generate theory for the purpose—in order to be able to predict the effect of such change. Attention will have to be directed to the diffusion and dissemination of change manifestations. The spatial organization of the society is salient in this context, and questions need to be raised concerning the interdependence and intercommunication of regions and geographical areas. In doing this, the Evaluator will also be attentive to the appropriateness of such diffusion and dissemination to a particular region (on the basis of the values, assumptions, goal images present in the region) and to the capacity of the region for undergoing fundamental change while preserving its proper basic nature. Given the execution of the first two tasks referred to above, the Evaluator should be prepared for carrying out this last concern, although the specific information may have to be refined.

Before concluding this section and chapter, the essay's focus on project evaluation needs to be resurrected. It might be argued that the concern with social change and societal transformation tends to drown out any specific reference to project output and impact. To some extent, this is true, except possibly in the case of very 'powerful', penetrating projects of considerable size. If this is so, the third to sixth sections inclusive would appear to be irrelevant, and the Evaluator might just as well identify and evaluate manifestations of fundamental social change (or note their absence). However, the careful tracing of project impacts and impacts of impacts allows the Evaluator and decision-maker to keep in touch, so to speak, with specific projects. It is easier to trace the contribution of specific projects to higher-order impacts and change manifestations, as suggested here, than it is to attempt to trace the causal chain or ramifications from higher-order change manifestations to specific project outputs.

Notes

1. From a systems perspective, the simple cause-and-effect relationship of traditional social science needs to be supplemented by the search for configurations of conditions that are likely to bring about effects (including effects of previous effects). The search is thus not for specific causal factors that are responsible for effects, and the traditional articulation of hypothesis in terms of independent-dependent varia-

bles and unidirectional forces cannot do justice to the complexity of socio-cultural phenomena.

2. It must be stressed again that we are here not espousing a political ideology. The metacriterion applies not to a specific political regime, but rather to the functioning of any kind of regime that is not dominated by people who think they are superhumans. While the ideals of democracy incorporate feedback processes and the mutual taking-into-account of multiple perspectives, practice does not in all respects live up to the ideal.
3. The motivations for these pleas may differ. At least some of the literature wants an early involvement on the part of the evaluator so that the latter may have an opportunity to make the evaluation situation better structured (in terms of clearly articulated goals and objectives, as well as the existence of controls) and thus more suitable for the application of his methods and techniques.
4. At least in practice. But Suchman (1967) did stress the importance of impact evaluation.
5. We are here referring to project outputs. As a socio-cultural system, the project engages not only in providing people with family-planning devices and advice. It puts out information about itself and its purpose; it sends money to suppliers; it may have to justify itself to political authorities. Any one of these outputs, as well as others, has effects on environmental structures and leaves differential impacts.
6. The questions of the impact of changes in one subsystem on other subsystems will be treated in the next section of this chapter. Here, direct effects of project output are considered.
7. 'Comprehensive' or 'integrated' projects or programmes pursue multiple interrelated goals. Unesco and other agencies have learned that the teaching of literacy needs to be supported by vocational education and the like if a meaningful and lasting impact is to be achieved.
8. A negative relation is of the following sort: the greater *A*, the smaller *B*, or the smaller *A*, the greater *B*. In a positive relation, both events move in the same direction: the greater *A*, the greater *B*, or the smaller *A*, the smaller *B*.

Epilogue

As is so often the case, the end of a treatise is at best a beginning. The true purpose of the preceding chapters has been to stimulate—to stimulate not only the author but the reader as well to try out perspectives with which he may not be familiar. The next several volumes have not yet been written; the author does not expect to write them, at least not by himself. At least two themes that are necessarily associated with the contents of this essay have been neglected, if not disregarded. They relate to the operationalization and application of the suggestions made in the essay, and to the organizational arrangements for the kind of evaluation sketched on the preceding pages. The successful treatment of these two themes is necessary to 'prove' the soundness of the present essay. We believe, of course, that such a treatment is possible, although it will take quite some time and much methodological innovation to routinize the approach. In the meantime, however, the thoughts expressed in this essay may prove to be specific enough to enter the practical world of development efforts in an informal, perhaps diffuse way.

The essay does not shirk complexity; on the contrary, it stresses the complexity of the real world. Social policy must be able to deal with the 'organized complexity' of social systems. What is suggested here is that we cannot afford to wait for the appropriate tools to evolve. Rather, the capacity to grasp and understand complexity is at stake. What is needed is a more generally pervading preparedness to incorporate and face complexity in our thinking and in our orientation to real-world problems. It is hoped that the conceptual-methodological treatment of this essay may have made a modest contribution to this end.

References

ACKOFF, R. L. 1974*a*. *Redesigning the Future: A Systems Approach to Societal Problems*. New York, Wiley & Sons.

——. 1974*b*. Beyond Problem Solving. In: *General Systems,* Part VI, Obiter Dicta, p. 237-9, Yearbook of the Society for General Systems Research, Vol. XIX, Washington, D.C.

ADELMAN, I.; MORRIS, C. T. 1967. *Society, Politics, and Economic Development: A Quantitative Approach*. Baltimore and London, The Johns Hopkins Press.

ASHBY, R. W. 1956. *An Introduction to Cybernetics*. London, Chapman & Hall; New York, Science Editions, John Wiley & Sons, 1963.

BACHRACH, P. 1977. Evaluating Development Programmes: A Synthesis of Recent Experience. Paris, OECD Development Centre (mimeo). (Experiences in Rural Development, Occasional Paper No. 3, CD/R(77)29.)

BEER, S. 1972. *Brain of the Firm*. New York, Herder & Herder.

BENNETT, C. A.; LUMSDAINE, A. A. (eds.). 1975. *Evaluation and Experiment: Some Critical Issues Assessing Social Programs*. New York, Academic Press.

——. 1975. Assessing Alternative Conceptions of Evaluation. In: Bennett and Lumsdaine.

BENNIS, Warren. 1966. *Changing Organizations*. New York, McGraw-Hill.

BERNSTEIN, I. N. 1978. Social Control in Applied Social Science: A Study of Evaluative Researchers' Conformity to Technical Norms. *Social Science Research,* Vol. 7, March, p. 24-47.

BERNSTEIN, I. N.; FREEMAN, H. E. 1975. *Academic and Entrepreneurial Research: The Consequences of Diversity in Federal Evaluation Studies*. New York, Russell Sage Foundation.

BUCKLEY, W. 1967. *Sociology and Modern Systems Theory*. Englewood Cliffs, N.J., Prentice-Hall. (Prentice-Hall Sociology Series.)

CALABRESI, G.; BOBBITT, P. 1978. *Tragic Choices*. New York, W. W. Norton. (The Fels Lectures on Public Policy Analysis.)

CAMPBELL, D. T. 1969. Reforms as Experiments, *American Psychologist,* Vol. 24, No. 4, p. 409-29.

CAMPBELL, D. T.; STANLEY, J. C. 1963. *Experimental and Quasi-Experimental Designs for Research*. Chicago, Ill., Rand McNally.

CHODAK, S. 1973. *Societal Development: Five Approaches with Conclusions from Comparative Analysis*. New York, Oxford University Press.

CHURCHMAN, C. W. 1968. *The Systems Approach*. New York, Dell Publishing Company. (A Delta Book.)

CHURCHMAN, C. W. 1971. *The Design of Inquiring Systems: Basic Concepts of Systems and Organization*. New York and London, Basic Books.

DEUTSCH, K. W. 1961. Social Mobilization and Political Development. *The American Political Science Review*, Vol. LV, No. 3, p. 439-514.

——. 1964. Communication Theory and Political Integration. In: P. E. Jacob and J. V. Toscano (eds.), *The Integration of Political Communities*, p. 46-74. Philadelphia and New York, J. B. Lippincott.

——. 1966*a*. *The Nerves of Government: Models of Political Communication and Control*. With a New Introduction. New York, The Free Press.

——. 1966*b*. *Nationalism and Social Communication*. 2nd ed. Cambridge, Mass., The M.I.T. Press.

——. 1977. Toward Drift Models and Steering Models. In: K. W. Deutsch, B. Fritsch, H. Jaguaribe and A. S. Markovits (eds.), *Problems of World Modeling: Political and Social Implications*, p. 5-10. Cambridge, Mass., Ballinger Publishing Company.

DEUTSCH, K. W.; MERRITT, R. L. 1965. Effects of Events on National and International Images. In: H. C. Kelman (ed.), *International Behavior: A Social-Psychological Analysis*, p. 130-87. New York, Holt, Rinehart & Winston. (Published for the Society for the Psychological Study of Social Issues.)

DUPREE, L. 1970. *Free Enterprise in Afghanistan*. New York, American Universities Field Staff. (Report XIV: 6.)

FARVAR, M. T.; MILTON, J. P. (eds.). 1972. *The Careless Technology: Ecology and International Development*. Garden City, N.Y., The Natural History Press. (The Record of the Conference on the Ecological Aspects of International Development convened by the Conservation Foundation and the Center for the Biology of Natural Systems, Washington University. 8-11 December 1968, Airlie House, Warrenton, Va.)

FINSTERBUSCH, K. 1977. The Potential Role of Social Impact Assessments in Instituting Public Policies. In: K. Finsterbusch and C. P. Wolf (eds.) 1977. *Methodology of Social Impact Assessment*. Stroudsburg, Pa., Dowden, Hutchinson & Ross. (Community Development Series, CDS/32.)

FINSTERBUSCH, K.; WOLF, C. P. (eds.) 1977. *Methodology of Social Impact Assessment*. Stroudsburg, Pa., Dowden, Hutchinson & Ross. (Community Development Series, CDS/32.)

FLODEN, R. E.; WEINER, S. S. 1978. Rationality to Ritual: The Multiple Roles of Evaluation in Governmental Processes. *Policy Sciences*, Vol. 9, p. 9-18.

FRIEDMAN, J. 1969. The Guyana Program in a Regional Perspective. In: Lloyd Rodwin and Associates, *Planning Urban Growth and Regional Development: The Experience of the Guyana Program of Venezuela*, p. 147-59. Cambridge, Mass., The M.I.T. Press.

GILBERT, J. P.; LIGHT R. L.; MOSTELLER, F. 1975. Assessing Social Innovations: An Empirical Base for Policy. In: C. A. Bennett and A. A. Lumsdaine (eds.) 1975. *Evaluation and Experiment: Some Critical Issues Assessing Social Programs*, p. 39-135. New York, Academic Press.

GONZÁLEZ CASANOVA, P. 1970. *Las categorías del desarrollo económico y la investigación en ciencias sociales*. 2nd ed. Mexico City, Universidad Autónoma de México. (Instituto de Investigaciones Sociales.)

GORDON, G.; MORSE, E. V. 1975. Evaluation Research. In: Alex Inkeles, James Coleman and Neil Smelser, *Annual Review of Sociology*, Vol. 1.

GROSS, B. M. 1966. The State of the Nation: Social Systems Accounting. In: R. A. Bauer (ed.), *Social Indicators*, p. 154-271. Cambridge, Mass., The M.I.T. Press. (Technology, Space, and Society. Series Prepared by the American Academy of Arts and Sciences.)

GUTTENTAG, M.; STRUENING, E. L. (eds.). 1975. *Handbook of Evaluation Research*, Vol. 2. Beverly Hills, Calif., Sage Publications.

HAGE, J. 1974. *Communication and Organizational Control: Cybernetics in Health and Welfare Settings.* New York, John Wiley & Sons. (A Wiley-Interscience Publication.)

HAMBLIN, R. L.; JACOBSEN, R. B.; MILLER, J. L.-L. 1973. *A Mathematical Theory of Social Change.* New York, John Wiley & Sons. (A Wiley-Interscience Publication.)

HAYES, Jr, S. P. 1959. *Evaluating Development Projects.* 2nd ed. rev., Paris, Unesco, 1969.

HOLT, R. T.; JOB, B. L.; MARKUS, L. 1978. Catastrophe Theory and the Study of War. *The Journal of Conflict Resolution,* Vol. XXII, No. 2, June, p. 171-208.

IGLESIAS, G. U. (ed.) 1976. *Implementation: The Problem of Achieving Results: A Casebook on Asian Experiences.* Manila, Eastern Regional Organization for Public Administration.

LIKERT, Rensis. 1967. *The Human Organization.* New York, McGraw-Hill.

MARUYAMA, M. 1963. The Second Cybernetics: Deviation Amplifying Mutual Causal Processes. *Amercian Scientist,* Vol. 51, p. 164-79.

——. 1977. Heterogenistics: An Epistemological Restructuring of Biological and Social Sciences. *Cybernetica,* Vol. 20, No. 1, p. 69-86.

MEADOWS, D. *et al.* 1972. *The Limits to Growth: A Report for the Club of Rome's Project on the Predicament of Mankind.* New York, Universe Books. (A Potomac Associates Book.)

MILLER, J. G. 1978. *Living Systems.* New York, McGraw-Hill.

MITROFF, I. I. 1974. *The Subjective Side of Science: A Study of the Apollo Moon Scientists.* New York, American Elsevier.

MITROFF, I. I.; FEATHERINGHAM, T. R. 1974. On Systemic Problem Solving and the Error of the Third Kind. *Behavioral Science,* Vol. 19, No. 6, November, p. 383-93.

MITROFF, I. I.; SAGASTI, F. 1973. Epistemology as General Systems Theory: An Approach to the Design of Complex Decision-Making Experiments. *Philosophy of the Social Sciences,* Vol. 3, p. 117-34.

MOORE, F. J. 1977. Development Considered: Four Simple Notes on a Common Theme. *Focus: Technical Cooperation,* p. 19-22, Supplement to *International Development Review,* Vol. XIX, No. 4.

MORRIS, M. D.; LISER, F. B. 1977. The PQLI: Measuring Progress in Meeting Human Needs. *Communique* (Overseas Development Council, Washington, D.C.), No. 32.

OLSEN, M. E.; MERWIN, D. 1977. Toward a Methodology for Conducting Social Impact Assessments Using Quality of Social Life Indicators. In: K. Finsterbusch and C. P. Wolf (eds.) 1977. *Methodology of Social Impact Assessment,* p. 43-63. Stroudsburg, Pa., Dowden, Hutchinson & Ross. (Community Development Series, CDS/32.)

PATTON, M. Q. 1978. *Utilization-Focused Evaluation.* Beverly Hills, Cal., Sage Publications.

——. 1975. *Alternative Evaluation Research Paradigm.* Grand Forks, N.D., University of North Dakota, North Dakota Study Group on Evaluation.

PATTON, M. Q. et al. 1977. In Search of Impact: An Analysis of the Utilization of Federal Health Evaluation Research. In: C. H. Weiss (ed.), *Using Social Research in Public Policy Making.* Lexington, Mass., Lexington Books.

RASTOGI, P. N. 1977. Societal Development as the Quintessence of World Development. In: K. W. Deutsch, B. Fritsch, H. Jaguaribe and A. S. Markovits (eds.), *Problems of World Modeling: Political and Social Implications,* p. 339-77. Cambridge, Mass., Ballinger Publishing Co.

RONDINELLI, D. A. 1978. *Bicol River Basin Urban Functions in Rural Development Project: Summary and Evaluation.* Washington, D.C. Office of Urban Development Support Bureau, Agency for International Development, United States Department of State. (Contract No. AID/ta-C-1356.)

ROSSI, P. G. 1972. Boobytraps and Pitfalls in the Evaluation of Social Action Programs. In: C. H. Weiss (ed.), *Evaluating Action Programs.* Boston, Mass., Allyn & Beacon.

ROSSI, P. H.; WRIGHT, S. 1977. Evaluation Research: An Assessment of Theory, Practice and Politics, *Evaluation Quarterly*, Vol. 1, p. 5-52.

RUTMAN, L. 1977. Planning an Evaluation Study; Formative Research and Program Evaluability. In: L. Rutman (ed.), *Evaluation Research Methods: A Basic Guide*, Chapters 1 and 3. Beverly Hills, Calif., and London, Sage Publications. (Sage Focus Edition, Vol. 3.)

SUCHMAN, E. A. 1967. *Evaluative Research: Principles and Practice in Public Service and Social Action Programs*. New York, Russell Sage Foundation.

THOM, R. 1975. *Structural Stability and Morphogenesis*. Reading, Mass., W. A. Benjamin. (Original: *Stabilité structurelle et morphogenèse*, 1972.)

TRAVIESO, F. 1976. ¿Ciudad Guayana, polo de desarrollo? In: *Ensayos sobre planificación regional del desarrollo*, p. 469-76. Compiled by the Latin American Institute of Economic and Social Planning and the Division of Social Development of the United Nations, Mexico City, Siglo Veintiuno Editores.

WATKINS, G. A. 1977. Development of a Social Impacts Assessment Methodology (SIAM). In: K. Finsterbusch and C. P. Wolf (eds.) 1977. *Methodology of Social Impact Assessment*, p. 35-42. Stroudsburg, Pa., Dowden, Hutchinson & Ross. (Community Development Series, CDS/32.)

WEAVER, J. H.; JAMESON, K. P.; BLUE, R. N. 1978. Growth and Equity: Can They Be Happy Together? *Development: International Development Review* (Rome), Vol. XX, No. 1, p. 20-7.

WEISS, C. H. 1972 *a*. *Evaluation Research: Methods of Assessing Program Effectiveness*. Englewood Cliffs, N.J., Prentice-Hall. (Prentice-Hall Methods of Social Science Series.)

——. 1972*b*. Evaluating Educational and Social Action Programs: A 'Treeful of Owls'. In: C. H. Weiss (ed.), *Evaluating Action Programs*. Boston, Mass., Allyn & Beacon.

WHANG, I.-J. 1976. Implementation of the National Family Planning Program of Korea: 1962-1971. In: G. U. Iglesias (ed.) 1976. *Implementation: The Problem of Achieving Results: A Case-book on Asian Experiences*, p. 309-36. Manila, Eastern Regional Organization for Public Administration.

WHITE, W. T. 1977. Yaquina Bay: A Case Study in Social Impact Assessment. In: K. Finsterbusch and C. P. Wolf (eds.) 1977. *Methodology of Social Impact Assessment*, p. 35-42. Stroudsburg, Pa., Dowden, Hutchinson & Ross. Community Development Series, CDS/32.)

WICKHAM, W. A. 1978. Small Farmers: To Serve the Client, Know the Client. *RF (The Rockefeller Foundation) Illustrated*, Vol. 4, No. 2, September, p. 4-5.

WYNIA, G. W. 1972. *Politics and Planners: Economic Development Policy in Central America*. Madison, Wis., The University of Wisconsin Press.

ZAHLER, R. S.; SUSSMAN, H. J. 1977. Claims and Accomplishments of Applied Catastrophe Theory. *Nature*, Vol. 269, No. 27, p. 759-63.

ZEEMAN, E. E. 1976. Catastrophe Theory. *Scientific American*, Vol. 234, No. 4, p. 65-83.

[B.20] SS.78/D109/A